# MONEY MATTERS

## Spiritual Foundation, Principles & Practical Application

### PATRICK MURIITHI NYAGA

In all the time I have known Patrick Nyaga, I have never doubted where his spiritual instincts and loyalties lay: with God. *Money Matters* is based on solid biblical teaching. As with his other books, his intentions are pastoral, to assist people to overcome sinful habits and barriers. In this book, he addresses money issues. I heartily recommend this book to anyone who would want to glean gems of wisdom in dealing with money as they journey with God.

**Prof. Misheck Nyirenda**
Global Translation Advisor, United Bible Societies

Having known Apostle Patrick all his life, I identify strongly with the personal examples in his book, *Money Matters: Spiritual Foundation, Principles & Practical Application*. Written in his characteristic simple and fun style, the book is enlightening and inspiring. There is a unique blending of theological insight of the apostle, and the practical wisdom of the accountant, the two hats Patrick wears with mastery. The principles shared in the book, if followed, will liberate you from financial strongholds and put you on a path of financial peace and fulfillment.

**Dr Sammy Gitaari**
Founder & Bishop, Gospel Celebration Church, Kenya

Patrick Muriithi Nyaga truly walks in favour with God and men. He has a magnetic way about him that draws people and makes everyone he comes in contact with feel blessed, encouraged, and inspired. Reading through the principles and the practical application Patrick has put down in this book, the reader will receive help on how to break financial strongholds. I recommend *Money Matters* for anyone who wants to enjoy financial freedom.

**Pastor Steve Collins**
Church Eleven32, Dallas, Texas

Apostle Patrick Muriithi Nyaga is a seasoned man of God who walks in the apostolic anointing and calling. In this book, he is telling the reader the difference between wealth and money, and the impact they both can have in one's life. *Money Matters* is for everyone and a must-read for those in full-time ministry.

**Dr Collins C. Chipaya**
Founder & Apostle, Revival Fire Missions International, Zambia

By reading this book, I have learned to value what I have and make it worthwhile for the glory of God. Thank you for this great inspiration. This is a must-read for all.

**Karimi A. Njeru**
Magistrate

*Money Matters: Spiritual Foundation, Principles & Practical Application* is a prophetic message to our generation. It contains spiritual, practical, and proven financial principles that have worked and are demonstrated in the life of the author. The lifestyle of Apostle Patrick is proof that these principles work. I recommend this book to every person set for a financial turnaround.

**Prophet Paul Mwaniki**
Senior Pastor, Glory Christian Church, Kenya

Patrick Muriithi Nyaga has given us access to a deep and yet practical understanding of the Bible that the Lord has so graciously bestowed upon his life and ministry. Perusing through the pages of this book made me feel like I was sitting in a class where he was teaching on financial freedom. I highly recommend *Money Matters* especially to preachers, and to every believer who seeks to walk in the fullness of God's blessings.

**Apostle James Mbugua**
Senior Elder, Fountain Gate Church & Relating Ministries, Kenya

I have observed the ministry life of Apostle Patrick Nyaga and confirm he is the right person to teach on the subject of money. The author has done a good job expounding the Scriptures while providing life-changing stories. I endorse *Money Matters: Spiritual Foundation, Principles & Practical Application* as a tool for equipping the church in our day to rise and gain wealth for kingdom advancement.

**Dr David Juma**
Apostle, Life Church International, Kenya

In *Money Matters: Spiritual Foundation, Principles & Practical Application*, Apostle Patrick Muriithi Nyaga passionately delivers a timely, relevant, cross-cultural and trans-generational, message born from his heart. This practical and insightful book skillfully combines theology and practice, interweaving both biblical principles and real-life testimonies. Here is a book on financial freedom from an author who lives his message. You will certainly yearn for more! I recommend this book to every believer and especially those in ministry.

**Rev Samson Muniu**
Lead Pastor, Victory Chapel, Dallas, Texas.

This book is an invaluable tool for assisting every reader make key decisions on matters relating to money. Patrick provides us with the keys to unlock our hearts and minds from the bondage of poverty, not by a "get-rich" teaching, but by partnering with God to manage our finances. Having the right attitude towards wealth and money will remove the veil from our creative imagination and allow God to free us from the myths and attitudes we have about money. I endorse this book and recommend it to everyone who wants to have a mind shift and transformation to view money as a spiritual resource.

**Bishop Jackson Kingori**
Founder, Neema Gospel Church, Dallas, Texas

This book is a must-read for all who endeavor to live a productive life enjoying financial liberty with kingdom-based principles.

**Evangelist Noel Ngure**
Founder, Beyond Horizons International &
Daughters of Faith Ministries
USA

Apostle Patrick expounds in a simple yet profound manner the spiritual and practical aspects of money. His life is an example that the principles work. Patrick has a unique grace to teach about money with anointing, validated by the many testimonies of those he has ministered to. Read Money Matters as a manual, alongside the Bible, for Kingdom economics (kingdomnomics).

**Dr Patrick Kariuki**
Founder and Bishop, Great Gospel Visioner International, Kenya.

# MONEY MATTERS

## SPIRITUAL FOUNDATION PRINCIPLES & PRACTICAL APPLICATION

PATRICK MURIITHI NYAGA

PUBLISHING
Institute of Africa

MONEY MATTERS: Spiritual Foundation, Principles & Practical Application
Copyright © 2017 Patrick Muriithi Nyaga

Revised and updated 2020



ISBN 13: 978-9966-69-045-6

This edition published by:

Nairobi, Kenya.
www.publishing-institute.org
info@publishing-institute.org

Originally published by Integrity Publishers Inc.

# CONTENTS


Endorsements.................................................................ii

Foreword.....................................................................xiii

Preface ..................................................................... xv

## FOUNDATION

1 Spiritual Dimension of Money .................................3

2 Heart and Wealth .....................................................9

## PRINCIPLES

3 The Prayer of Jabez ................................................29

4 Develop Financial Integrity...................................37

5 Principles of Administering God's Resources.........47

6 The Harvest Mentality ...........................................53

## PRACTICAL APPLICATION

7 The Power of Giving................................................61

8 The Danger of Unmanaged Debt ...........................69

9 Limitations to Financial Breakthrough..................77

10 The Wisdom of Saving & Investing.......................87

11 Serve God with Money..........................................93

12 Truths and Half-truths about Money ................. 101

Conclusion .............................................................. 107

Notes ...................................................................... 109

About the Author ................................................... 111

*I dedicate this book to my departed dad—Junius Nyaga, who labored much to see his son empowered to break some financial strongholds.*

*Though he never lived to enjoy the fruits of his labor in my life, I remain indebted to him.*

# SPECIAL THANKS TO:

My dear wife, Pastor Grace Muriithi, and our children, Jewel, Moses, and Collins. Grace, you have walked with me on this journey and have been patient with me as I fought through hard financial seasons.

Dr Kirimi Barine, you encouraged me to write my first book, *Called to Serve*, when many people thought it was not doable. With three more out and more on the way, I remain indebted to you, sir.

Purity Murungi, from your busy schedule you spared some time to go through this book and give your critique. May the Lord bless you.

Esther Nyaga, I highly appreciate your editorial contribution to this book.

Nancy Nelson Garcia, you worked so hard despite your busy schedule to edit this book. May God bless you.

Apostle Dr Collins Chipaya, you have prayed for me and practically showed me how to break financial strongholds and limitations, including through giving. I honor you, Dad.

Finally, the family of Gospel Celebration Church, Kayole. You gave me a chance to teach you almost all the principles written in this book. God bless you all.

The King James Version of the Bible mentions the word money 140 times. If we include words like gold, silver, wealth, riches, inheritance, debt, poverty, and other related topics, we discover the Bible pays a great deal of attention to financial matters—more than nearly any other subject. It doesn't just mention the word money; the Bible goes on to provide answers to the issues people struggle with on the subject.

Grandich, the author of *Confessions of a Wall Street Whiz Kid*, says, "I get my financial guidance from the Bible. Money and possessions are the second most referenced topic in the Bible—money is mentioned more than 800 times—and the message is clear: Nowhere in Scripture is debt viewed in a positive way."

*Money Matters: Spiritual Foundation, Principles & Practical Application* attempts to deal with money issues from a biblical perspective by providing the spiritual foundation of money and providing practical tips for everyday life use. A person's underlying philosophy about who owns their money influences their relationship with money. If you believe that God owns everything and you are but a steward of His resources, then what God says guides how you relate with money; how you give, save, invest, and even deal with debt.

Although the emphasis of this work is on biblical principles of money, it contains practical examples from the author's life that must be understood in the context they happened for you to make sense of them. Also, in appreciation of the diversity of our theological persuasions and interpretations, it is okay to disagree with the author's perspective on any matter.

Should this happen, the book provides a platform for a healthy discourse. Having known the author for many years, his passion to be biblically correct in his interpretation of the Scriptures is not in doubt.

I hope you will get some insights from this book to help you broaden your perspective on money from God's Word, develop financial integrity, serve God with the resources He has entrusted to you, and manage any debt you might have.

**Dr Kirimi Barine,**

**Nairobi, Kenya**

Whenever I minister and pray for individual or congregational needs, this prayer request always tops the list—pray for a financial breakthrough!

But what does financial breakthrough mean? Does it imply a salary increment or an extra source of income? Could it be debt cancellation or perhaps stronger purchasing power?

Harold Herring, in his article *7 Keys To Your Financial Breakthrough*, defines breakthrough as the "Sudden burst of revelation that enthusiastically moves you beyond all previous points of past resistance bringing you to a new level of success."

Financial breakthrough to one person could mean securing a job. For another, it is when a spouse gets employed, while to another, it is when their business flourishes. For a pastor, a financial breakthrough could be when membership increases or tithes and offerings improve.

I once watched an interview with the managing director of Equity Bank, a leading indigenous Kenyan bank. The elated interviewer kept saying, "I can't believe that I am seated next to a billionaire." Perhaps the managing director was embarrassed by the continuous repetition of the statement, or maybe he just decided to address the issue once and for all. So, he asked the interviewer, "What would you do with a billion shillings?"

The interviewer seemed unprepared for the question, and her response was she would just use it to help people. The managing director then said, "God gives every person enough to spend on their regular bills." That is to say, if you have billions in revenue, you probably have billions in expenses, and vice versa for the person with little.

After one of my speaking engagements, a lady asked me to pray for her to get a job that would give her $300, promising she would give to God and my ministry if her prayer was answered. Not long after that prayer, her salary rose to $400; I know this because she called to tell me. Our paths did not cross for quite some time after that. When we finally met, she shared with me yet again how badly she needed a financial breakthrough. The lady had forgotten she was earning more than we had prayed for earlier, and had not yet fulfilled her promise to give to God and my ministry, even though she had reached and surpassed her original financial breakthrough desire.

I define financial breakthrough as a point where one becomes rich, not because they have money, but because they have broken a financial stronghold or limitation. Dale Robbins, writing about breaking spiritual strongholds, says that the word stronghold doesn't necessarily refer to something as extreme as demon possession, but can merely be a strong influence or grip, persistent oppression, obsessions, hindrances or harassment; implying that one can have a stronghold over finances.

There is a time when a prayer for fare or food to eat is such a serious need in the life of a person. The individual then gets to a place where they break that limitation and are able to believe within their hearts that food and fare is already provided for. Kings and heads of state rarely carry hard cash, yet can command things that require money, and they get done. Every believer has received the power to become a son of God through the spirit of adoption and to become kings with

Him. This is why we reign in the heavenly realms with Christ Jesus our Lord and King (Ephesians 2:6). Just like a king, it is possible to break strongholds and limitations to the point where one can make purchases without any money in the pocket ("...and you who have no money, come, buy and eat! Come buy wine and milk without money...", Isaiah 55:1).

When God said, "Let us make mankind in our own image, in our likeness..." (Genesis 1:26), the intent was to look like God and function like Him. This is what man lost when he sinned. When an individual reconciles with God, God restores His image and the power to transact as He does. When I was in college, there were days I did not have money for transport. One morning, I left the house early and by faith, stood at the bus stop, believing God for a miracle of a free ride to the city center. It so happened a young bus conductor saw me, called me by my name, and invited me to enter the bus. He then told me that as long as I saw his vehicle, I had a free ride to or from the city center. You can imagine my delight, I didn't know him, but since he had called me by my name, I was not worried and took his offer. We did not have another conversation except for the usual morning or evening greetings. One day, while waiting for the bus to fill up, the conductor sat next to me, and we got talking. He asked how my brother Wanjohi was. At the mention of the name, I knew something was amiss, for I did not have a brother called Wanjohi. We talked some more, and we discovered that the conductor had mistaken me for his friend's brother. How my name and image and that of his friend's brother resembled only God knows! If someone's image got me carried for free for almost a year, how much more do you think the image of God will do for you?

Two people can walk into a shop to purchase an item. One may present a check and walk away with the item, while the other, his pleas notwithstanding, will be asked to collect the item once his check has cleared.

This book's goal is to help you realize that until you defeat the 'enemy' called poverty, you cannot enjoy financial freedom.

Different people interpret the state of poverty differently. A poor man in one place could be the richest in another location. In other words, no matter your financial status, there will always be someone who is poorer than you, and another who is richer. The rich person you admire is ahead of you because he or she has broken some strongholds you have so far not broken. As you read through this book, I pray that you will discover and deal with whatever has hindered your financial breakthrough.

FOUNDATION

# CHAPTER ONE

# THE SPIRITUAL DIMENSION OF MONEY

When you walk around the city of Nairobi, it is common to see beggars asking for alms. I used to give them money until I realized that giving them handouts was not solving the problem. It only raised their begging level! In my opinion, there is no amount of money that can eradicate poverty. No wonder when Judas argued that the expensive oil Mary used to anoint Jesus' feet should have been sold to help the poor, Jesus said, "…the poor will always be with you" (John 12:8). Poverty is deeper than lack, to deal with it, anointing has to be involved.

Luke 4:18 spells out Christ's mission statement. He said, "The Spirit of the Lord is on me, because He has anointed me to proclaim good news to the poor. He has sent me to proclaim freedom for the prisoners and recovery of sight for the blind, to set the oppressed free." This verse captures the reason and the proof of Christ's anointing.

It is important to note that the same anointing Jesus needed to heal the sick, open the eyes of the blind, and to set free those in captivity, was the same anointing he needed to deal with poverty. The anointing of the Holy Spirit upon Jesus included proclaiming the good news to the poor.

When you take a closer look at this verse, it is tempting to think Jesus was not fair to the poor. The prisoners and the oppressed would need freedom, while the blind would need sight. Wouldn't the poor then need money as opposed to good news? My understanding of this statement by Jesus is that poverty is not just a money issue but a spiritual and mindset issue..

Phil Pringle, in *Keys to Financial Excellence*, says, "Poverty is more a state of mind than a state of life. You will find that people with a poverty mindset walk around shops for half a day comparing prices only to save themselves a few dollars. If we think that saving five or ten dollars is worth half a day's effort, then we are living in a poverty mindset".

The world is full of people who have money, yet are very poor. If we are to receive a financial breakthrough, we must appreciate the following principles.

## MONEY HAS A SPIRITUAL DIMENSION

I know a pastor friend whose grandfather and father were witch doctors. His family believed and practiced witchcraft. The witch doctor would ask all the people who went to him for help to put any amount of money in a certain horn before listening to their issues. He would not touch that money even when he was broke—the money acted as a "file" for all his customers. Thus every time he needed cash, he would shake this horn as he chanted, "Let the problems of the owners of this money come back. Let their problems come back!" Before long, the problems would surely return, and his customers would find their way back to him. To handle money appropriately, we must understand its spiritual dimension. "The natural person does not receive the things of the Spirit of God… because they are spiritually discerned"(1 Corinthians 2:14, NKJV).

There are people who live in poverty because evil powers have a hold on their "files". It is equally important to know how to tell your money is under attack. "For though we walk in the flesh, we do not war according to the flesh. For the weapons of our warfare are not carnal but mighty in God for pulling down strongholds" (1 Corinthians 10:3-4, NKJV).

When Christians handle their finances casually, the devil is happy because he can now use that as an opportunity to keep them in poverty. It is not uncommon to find individuals who are willing to bribe or trade sexual favours for employment, promotions, a better life, or in simple terms—more money.

One of the temptations the devil presented to Jesus had to do with wealth. "Again, the devil took him to a very high mountain and showed him all the kingdoms of the world and their splendor. 'All this I will give you,' he said, 'if you will bow down and worship me'" (Matthew 4:8-9). The devil delights in keeping a Christian in poverty because it presents a perfect foundation for temptation.

## EVIL ASSIGNMENTS

The enemy can interfere with a Christian's finances through what I would call evil assignments. There are people whose money is given evil assignments. As soon as they get their money, a sickness is sent to them or to relatives or friends they cannot ignore. It is important to check whether you see a pattern in this area. If at the end of the month or whenever you receive your income, something happens and you end up spending all your money on this one thing, it could be a spiritual cycle that requires breaking. Don't accept to live with it; it is an evil assignment over your money to make you poor and to deny you a chance to enjoy the fruit of your labor.

The Bible records that the Midianites would attack the Israelites to take away their harvest. In other words, the Midianites attacked the Israelites during the harvest season. No wonder Gideon was found hiding. "And there came an angel of the Lord, and sat under an oak which was in Ophrah... Gideon pressed wheat by the winepress to hide it from the Midianites" (Judges 6:11 KJV).

There are people who will only come to you in your harvest season. Every October-November in Kenya, the tea-growing areas are reportedly invaded by prostitutes, both male and female, as soon as the farmers receive their tea bonuses. These prostitutes strategically position themselves specifically for this period because there is money. In the same way, the enemy can assign agents to come for your money as soon as it hits your account, or it is in your pocket.

In the early '90s, my cousin developed an unusual problem. She would faint every end of the month when her father got paid. The family would rush her to the hospital in critical condition, but no sooner had my uncle spent all his money on her than she would wake up well. This continued for a long time, until God revealed that my uncle's money had been given an evil assignment. When the matter was handled spiritually, my cousin got healed and has never fainted since.

Some people ignorantly even thank God that bad events happened when they had money. Perhaps it is not a miracle, but an evil assignment on your money. Break the cycle through prayer so you can fully enjoy the work of your hands. Pray concerning your finances, for it is a spiritual matter that requires spiritual intervention.

## EVIL PROMISES

Evil promises are designed to delay, entice one to make wrong financial decisions, and in the end, cause hopelessness. A person can promise to employ you when in reality they know they have no vacancy. Others may promise to give you capital to start a business when they know they have no intention of honoring their promise. These false promises can contribute to wrong financial decisions that can lead to debt or loss.

Never spend a promise; wait for its realization and fulfillment. Let it find you moving on with your project rather than waiting and planning with what you cannot see. Do not put your hope on a man's promise; put your hope in God.

## EVIL MONITORS

Paul and Silas were strangers in Philippi but a lady who had a familiar spirit knew who they were. "These men are servants of the Most High God, who are telling you the way to saved." (Acts 16:17). Just as this lady could tell who Paul and Silas were, evil monitors can tell when a believer has money or when they start to prosper, seeking to sabotage their success. I have heard of believers who took out a loan and on the day they received it they are robbed. Others get the money to start a business and immediately lose their business through a strange fire, bad debts or rogue employees.

## EVIL DISTRACTIONS

Consistency and focus are key elements when dealing with finances. There are people who lose money because of the many voices speaking to them about what to do with their money. Have you seen people who take a loan with a certain business in mind only for them to get another business idea and start it? Many times they end up losing all their investments by not being single-minded.

It is important for a person to pray and hear God clearly on what they need to do. Not every good business is good for you. Only the one you have received breakthrough and peace from God.

## PRAYER

*Father in the name of Jesus Christ, I disconnect myself from any spiritual altar that speaks against my finances. I take authority in the power that is in the name of Jesus to declare that my finances belong to the altar of Jesus and not to any other altar.*

*Amen!*

# CHAPTER TWO

# HEART AND WEALTH

There is a great connection between the heart of a man and his wealth. The Bible says that where the treasure [wealth] of a man is, his heart is also there (Matthew 6:21). For a person to understand how to handle wealth, he must work on his or her heart. For as he thinks in his heart, so is he (Proverbs 23:7, NKJV). If your heart is convinced that you are poor, no amount of money can chase poverty, and if you are convinced you are rich, thoughts of poverty cannot get a space in your heart. You can never guard your heart from corruption if your wealth or money is not secure. Every believer must realize that his or her heart and their wealth are related.

Prosperity or poverty begins in the heart. "If you believe in your heart and confess with your mouth that Jesus is the Lord, then you shall be saved" (Romans 10:9). Salvation is about the heart. It is the same thing when it comes to matters of prosperity and poverty. If you can believe it you can have it. This is why it is very important to guard our hearts from feeding on the wrong information. "Keep your heart with all diligence; for out of it are the issues of life" (Proverbs 4:23, KJV). I would paraphrase and say, keep your heart with all diligence, for out of it springs the issues of prosperity or poverty.

When Moses was negotiating to have the children of Israel released, Pharaoh was ready to set them free on one condition; they could go, but without their flocks and herds (Exodus 10:24). This was their treasure. Pharaoh knew that holding their wealth was holding their hearts. Whoever holds your finances controls your heart and vice versa. This is the reason why the Lord Jesus came to give the good news to the poor: to enlighten the poor on their rights and to deliver their hearts from the hands of the enemy. For where your treasure is, there your heart will be also (Luke 12:34). Every time believers' money or wealth is held in someone's hand, their hearts too are held. The reverse is true: if one is in charge of their hearts, they will be in charge of their wealth. This also means that no matter how wealthy they become, their hearts will not be corrupted and their relationship with God will not be destroyed.

I have discovered the following secrets about wealth that I am persuaded every believer ought to know.

## WEALTH IS CREATED

Some people believe that there are those who were created to be poor and those who were created to be rich. That is a false belief. God is a rich Father, and He never created poor children. He is pleased to see his children flourish. That said, I believe that God expects us to create wealth not to 'pray wealth'.

I have also talked with people who believe that work is a curse from God since Adam's fall. This is not true. God works, and He created man after His nature and likeness. He worked for six days, and on the seventh day, He rested. In other words, before the curse, work was. Some people want to work for one day and rest for six days. It does not work that way. God set an example for humanity to follow.

It is important to note that work is not the only thing a person requires to make wealth. The Bible says it is God who gives us power to acquire wealth (Deuteronomy 8:18). This means that we must depend on God's help and power. Mere human efforts cannot break poverty.

If one has a wealth creation mentality, they will break their financial stronghold. You must see yourself as a creator and not just a consumer. We must pursue what we will leave behind for others instead of what others have left behind for us. In other words, we must move beyond propagating the "It's our time to eat" mentality. My prayer is that you would be a person who always looks for creating rather than consuming opportunities.

### *Wealth Creators Versus Wealth Consumers*

A person, who only thinks about how to spend money without considering how to use the dollar they have to make another, is a wealth consumer. On the other hand, a person who thinks about how to make a dollar out of another is a wealth creator. Wealth creators have an investor's mindset, while consumers have an eating mentality.

The following characteristics differentiate wealth consumers from wealth creators.

| Wealth creators | Wealth consumers |
| --- | --- |
| See a dollar in their hands as what brings in another dollar | Despise a dollar as something small without much value |
| Are problem solvers | Are problems themselves |
| Have value for time and do not waste it | Do not value time and seem to have it in excess |
| Are givers | Are borrowers |
| Sow their seed | Eat their seed |
| Despise free things | Look for free things |
| Have an established sleeping pattern | Sleep and wake up when they feel like |
| Are likely to have stable relationships | Are likely to have poor relationships |
| Are assets to humanity | Are liabilities to humanity |
| Have a saving culture and know the value of delayed/ deferred gratification | Spend all their money and are impulsive |

## WEALTH IS HIDDEN

*It is the glory of God to conceal a matter; to search out a matter is the glory of kings* (Proverbs 25:2).

Searching is an expression of a desire to know or to get something.

God is pleased when His people seek Him. When asked about why He spoke in parables, Jesus said, "Because the knowledge of the secrets of the kingdom of heaven has been given to you, but not to them" (Matthew 13:11).

To search out a matter involves two things: prayer and thinking. God did not just call us to pray, he also called us to think. God will never think on your behalf because He has given you His mind. Thinking right is as powerful as doing right. Carrying out a feasibility study is part of thinking. Many believers are quick to pray and start on their wealth creation journey with no room for research and consultation.

Consider the following areas where wealth is hidden and pray for wisdom and revelation to identify what belongs to you.

## PLACE

*The kingdom of heaven is like treasure hidden in a field. When a man found it, he hid it again, and then in his joy went and sold all he had and bought that field* (Matthew 13:44).

There is always a geographical area where God has ordained as your place for wealth. In as much as God is everywhere, He is also a territorial God. That is why He is called the God of Israel. When God asked Abraham to sacrifice his son Isaac, he was specific that it was to be on a mountain in the region of Moriah. On that mountain, God had had already provided for Abraham. If Abraham had missed on the mountain, he would have ended up killing his son. God created Adam and Eve and gave them a place called Eden. The promise of God to Abraham was about a place called Canaan. Elijah was told by God to go to a certain place for provision. There is always a place ordained by God for someone's prosperity. Just as you are not called to do everything or be everywhere, it is important to get a revelation of your place of wealth or prosperity. I am a firm believer that when a person fails to identify his place of prosperity, they risk an evil assignment on their money.

## PEOPLE

Every person reflects his or her networks. If you have a poor network, you will always remain poor. An individual may have a million dollars in his account, but his true wealth comes from his relationships. Jesus' strength was not in the money that Judas kept, but in his relationships. He had people like Nicodemus and Joseph of Arimathea who were men of means and had connections with the Roman government (Luke 23:50-53; John 19:38-42). He also had women who supplied His needs (Luke 8:2-3).

As you pray for resources, pray for divine relationships. If you are called by God to do God's work, then you must remember that you cannot achieve much if you do not invest in meaningful relationships. God has people ordained for you who may not be in your current circle of relationships; be open and follow His leading. Pray for your wealth destiny connectors. Saul needed Ananias to pray for him. In a vision, God sent him to pray for the restoration of Saul's sight (Acts 9). Believe God for a mentor. Pray that God connects you to a person who will help you reach your financial goals. He or she may not give you money but can be used by God greatly through ideas or connections.

## SECRETS

I believe that a person is as powerful as the secrets he or she keeps and as prosperous as the secrets he or she can handle. Samson's power and strength was in his hair. "If I be shaven, then my strength will go from me, and I shall become weak, and be like any other man" (Judges 16:17, KJV).

For God to trust you with His secrets, you must pass some tests. In John 15:15, Jesus tells His disciples, "I no longer call you servants but friends." In other words, Jesus is telling them He can trust them with secrets. Wealth is hidden in secret places (Isaiah 45:3), but you must be a friend of God to access His secrets.

A word of caution here is once God reveals his secrets to you, you must be careful who you share with. Samson tortured the Philistines for decades because he had a secret that no Philistine knew of. Each of the Philistine rulers had to pay Delilah 1100 shekels of silver to get the secret behind Samson's strength. "See if you could lure him into showing you the secret, of his great strength…Each one of us will give you eleven hundred shekels of silver." (Judges 16:5). He shared his secret, and it cost him his strength. Invest your time in God to get a secret that will work for you.

## WISDOM

Wisdom is key in money matters. The Bible says, *Wisdom is the principal thing; therefore get wisdom…* (Proverbs 4:7, NKJV). Once you receive revelation, pray for wisdom. Revelation requires wisdom for a successful outcome. Pharaoh had a dream, and Joseph interpreted it for him (Genesis 41). Revelation for Pharaoh came at the point when Joseph interpreted his dream. The revelation itself, however, was not sufficient. Pharaoh needed wisdom to know what to do with the revelation he had received. The reserve in the seven years of plenty was used to feed the people in the seven years of drought (Genesis 41:33-36). This is what wisdom does. It gives one the ability to turn a revelation into profit. Jacob got the revelation in a dream, in wisdom he negotiated for his cut (salary) from Laban, then he implemented the vision he had seen (Genesis 29; 30:31-33).

A wise person thinks outside the box. For example, a wise person views employment as a stepping stone to financial freedom. See employment as a school to learn, a source of capital, a point of connection and networking, and a place of exposure.

This does not mean undercutting your employer, for integrity is a key to one's financial breakthrough. When I worked as an accountant, I sold shoes on the side to my colleagues. I also discovered the power of networking by being open to meeting new people of like and different profession.

## WEALTH IS MINED

Treasures are never kept in an open place. You will not find gold, silver, diamonds, gemstones, or any other precious metals on the surface of the earth. They must be excavated or mined. A Christian 'mines' their wealth through:

**PRAYER**

God calls us to pray. When we pray, God reveals things that are unique, unsearchable and difficult to find in any other place prayer. *Call to Me and I will answer you, and I will tell you great and mighty things, which you do not know* (Jeremiah 33:3).

The power of a prayer is not about the volume, eloquence, tempo or how emotionally appealing it sounds. I have found that the effective prayer that avails much (James 5:16) has two key elements:

**Kingdom Agenda**

How does the kingdom of God benefit if your prayer is answered?

Hannah prayed to God for a son and promised that she would give the child back to God for His service (1 Samuel 1:11-28). Nehemiah prayed for favour with the king; for materials and permission to build the wall of Jerusalem (Nehemiah 1:4-11). Do you have a reason why you should be blessed with material things? How will the kingdom of God benefit with your wealth? How will the orphans and the poor benefit? Will you do God's work with your your wealth? If your answer to these questions is yes, then your prayer for wealth will avail much.

**Evidence**

How have you used the resources currently entrusted in your care? This has to do with faithfulness. God measures faithfulness by looking at two things: safety and increase. In the parable of the talents (Matthew 25:14-30), all the three servants returned to the owner the initial talents they had received.

The next level is the level of increase. God expects a faithful servant to produce a dollar from every dollar He puts in our hands. The master called the servant who did not multiply his talent, wicked and lazy, and took what he had because there was no increase.

Paul prayed for the Ephesians' eyes to be opened so that they could see the riches they had in Christ, *I pray that the eyes of your heart may be enlightened... to know...what are the riches of the glory of His inheritance in the saints* (Ephesians 1:18).

## WORK

Mahatma Gandhi lists wealth without work as one of his seven deadly sins. Many people would want to be rich but few want to work for their wealth. Cults, pyramid schemes and some network marketing companies prosper by propagating the idea that there is a short cut to wealth without work. Work and wealth are inseparable. Parents ought to teach this principle to their children, pastors to members, and leaders to citizens.

God created work and instructed Adam to work (Genesis 2:15). We do not work because of the curse. No! Work existed before the fall of man. Any person who does not work, no matter how much faith they have, cannot break their financial strongholds. James 2:17 says faith without works is dead; yet many believers have substituted work with faith. People who break financial strongholds never depend on chance or luck; they work hard.

Great ideas that bring about freedom from poverty develop as people work. As you put your hands and brain to work, wells of innovative wealth-creating ideas open and thus, strongholds are broken. I once told a friend I was too busy to carry out a certain task he'd requested. His response changed my mind. He said the reason he was sure I was the right person for the task was since I was too busy. He said, "If you want something done, give it to a busy person, for he has no room for procrastination." Bishop David Oyedepo, quoting Kim Woo Chong, the president of South Korean Daewoo Company said, "If you use your brain, it will develop." Many people say that they get more ideas when they go to a quiet place in the mountains or by the seaside, but actually, real ideas come only when the brain cells are working. In my case, I think best when I am working! What is more, creativity increases with hard work. As David Oyedepo says, "Those who work extremely hard can stretch their intuition and insight."

As one works, it is important to understand these two terminologies: 'working hard' and 'working smart.' Though very different, they are both important and must be used simultaneously. Those who work hard mostly depend on their physical strength while those who work smart depend on their mental strength. Naturally, smart workers have better returns and end up ruling over the 'hard' workers.

While waiting to catch a taxi in Nairobi, I saw a man pass by pulling an overloaded handcart and sweating copiously. He got stuck just where I was standing. The man asked me whether I would help push his handcart forward. This was quite an unusual request, but I found that I could not say no. As we walked, I asked how much the client would pay him for pushing such a heavy load. When he said an equivalent of $5, I knew he would need to eat, shower, and perhaps wear some nice clothes and cologne, all on his day's wages.

Later that day, I walked into a cosmetics shop where I found a popular brand of cologne going for $35. It dawned on me that although my handcart puller may need cologne to handle his body odor, he could not afford it. I compared this scenario with a manager who seats in an office signing checks all day. The manager in the office sweats less, is paid more, and can afford cologne while a handcart puller sweats more, yet cannot afford the much-needed cologne. Like King Solomon, I thought I had seen another evil under the sun. "One who sweats more cannot afford while one who sweats less can afford cologne."

In the Scriptures, we find an example of a smart worker: Caleb (Joshua 14 and 15). At 85 years old, Caleb asked Joshua to allow him to go for the mountains and fight the giants that inhabited them as his inheritance. He declared he was as strong as he had been 45 years earlier when he and his companions had spied out the land. You would think Caleb would face these giants head-on, especially after quoting his strength and age. When given the go-ahead to fight, Caleb offered his beautiful daughter as a price to the man who would capture the mountains for him. This is what I call working smart. Othniel took the challenge, killed the giants, and captured the land in exchange for a beautiful wife. I have no objection to hard work; I only say that as you work hard, work smart too.

## WEALTH HAS A PATTERN

Wealth follows a pattern. Spending time looking for the cause of a problem is better than doing the trial and error method. It takes less time, less resources, and the results are great. If we can identify the pattern, then we will flow in wealth. The pattern wealth typically follows includes:

## REVELATION

The term revelation comes from the word reveal. This means God reveals the hidden avenues for wealth to those who pray. God tells us to call to Him and He will show us great and unsearchable things we do not know (Jeremiah 33:3). A revelation from God will elevate you financially. It is not enough for a person to trust you with their credit or debit card if they don't trust you with their card PIN. When God begins to trust a person with His secrets, that person prospers (Proverbs 25:2).

God does not entrust his secrets to people who can't keep them. Many people are seekers of secrets but are not custodians of secrets.

Jacob worked for Laban for twenty years, during which time Laban changed his salary ten times. Whenever the speckled and spotted flock increased, Laban changed his deal. All through, no one knew Jacob's secret. Finally, when he left Laban, he disclosed to Rachel and Leah the secret of his prosperity. "In breeding season, I once had a dream in which I looked up and I saw…" (Genesis 31:10). We see Jacob sharing with his wives his revelation and implementation plan (Genesis 30:37-43).

People invest their time seeking for a revelation, but when they receive it, they do little or nothing about it. Whoever implements a revelation has more blessings than the one who receives a revelation and does not implement it.

## FAVOUR

Revelation directs you to where your wealth is, but favour helps you to get it. Hard labor without favour can never prosper an individual. It is possible to be where resources are and you don't enjoy them. Merely receiving a revelation about wealth does not mean you will acquire the wealth.

Although Nehemiah was the king's cupbearer, known to the king and trusted by him, he did not bank on his years of service when he wanted permission and resources to build the wall of Jerusalem. He prayed for favour (Nehemiah 1). Favour will make people release wealth to you without looking at your weaknesses or shortcomings. They will buy from your shop though there are many other shops because of favour. Esther found favour with the king and became a queen in a foreign land although she was a Jew (Esther 2). Ruth prayed for favour as she went to glean and received a harvest even though she had not planted in that land. Although she was a Moabitess, Ruth found favour with Boaz, a Jew, eventually marrying him (Ruth 2). Favour quickens wealth, breaks barriers, and brings ownership. Pray for God's favour upon the work of your hands.

## TIME AND SEASONS

The Bible talks about the sons of Issachar who understood the times and knew what Israel should do (1 Chronicles 12:32). Wealth follows times and seasons. Every season has its wealth in it. Unless one can discern a season and know what to do in that season, they will miss the wealth in it. It is not about whether the external circumstances are good or bad, but about the ability to discern the season and know what to do. Romans 8:28 tells us that all things work together for good to those who love the Lord. I would interpret it this way: all seasons are meant to prosper those who understand what to do. Joseph understood what to do in the time of plenty to help Egypt prosper in the time of famine. Isaac too found himself in the land of the Philistines during famine. Instead of going to Egypt like his father Abraham had done before, God commanded Jacob to stay.

*Now there was a famine in the land—besides the previous famine in Abraham's time—and Isaac went to Abimelech king of the Philistines in Gerar. The LORD appeared to Isaac and said, "Do not go down to*

*Egypt; live in the land where I tell you to live. Stay in this land for a while, and I will be with you and will bless you…* (Genesis 26:1-3)

Jacob's prosperity was not just in him staying in Philistine, but knowing what to do there. In addition to Isaac obeying the Lord's command, he was sensitive to the demand of the season. He took action: he planted.

*Now Isaac sowed seed in the land, and in that very year he reaped a hundredfold. And the LORD blessed him, and he became richer and richer, until he was exceedingly wealthy. He owned so many flocks and herds and servants that the Philistines envied him* (Genesis 26:12-13).

You may be experiencing lack because you keep missing your season: the set time of your prosperity. You can tell you are in your season if you are at peace about implementing an idea even when it looks awkward in the eyes of others, that is, planting during drought. As the people of sight wait for the clouds to form, the person of faith plants without the sign of the clouds and reaps a harvest in due time. *Whoever watches the wind will not plant; whoever looks at the clouds will not reap* (Ecclesiastes 11:4)

**PROPHETIC VOICE**

We must not take the words of God's prophets and servants casually. *And my God will meet with all your needs according to the riches of his glory in Christ Jesus* (Philippians 4:19). When people obey the voice of God, the Lord meets their needs. He becomes their supplier and prospers them.

God's prophets speak the mind of God to his people, which includes prosperity (2 Chronicles 20:20). A prophet is able to decode the mind of God and proclaim it to the people. When a Levite accepted Micah's offer to be his personal priest for a pay of food, clothes, and a small salary, Micah said. "Now I know that the Lord will prosper me…" (Judges 17:13, ESV). Though Micah was an idol worshiper, he knew that a prophet of God has the power to bring prosperity to the people through prophetic declarations and teachings. "So the elders of the Jews continued to build and to prosper under the preaching of Haggai the prophet and Zachariah…" (Ezra 6:14). Honor your priest, prophet or pastor, that is, the person who takes care of your spiritual issues, for he carries a word of prosperity for you.

## GIVING

One key to kingdom prosperity is giving. Giving is not bribing God, nor is it supporting Him. It is not loaning God. Giving is simply obeying God's command and being like Him. God is a giver; therefore, His children must resemble Him by giving. Giving is not God's way of raising money but raising men. When you release money and stop treating it as more precious than God's word then God becomes your treasure and prosperity becomes your portion. *Relax your grip on your money and abandon your gold-plated luxury. God Almighty will be your treasure, more wealth than you can imagine* (Job 22:24-25, MSG). Giving attracts real wealth.

## WEALTH IS TRANSFERRED

Money and wealth are transferred to believers when they mature in God. There are things God will not transfer to a believer, just like there are things a father will not entrust to their underage child until he is mature. It doesn't matter the value of your offering to God, or how long you pray and fast, if you are not mature, you will not have wealth transferred to you. Galatians 4:1-2 (NKJV) says, "Now I say that the heir, as long as he is a child, does not differ at all from a slave, though he is master of all, but is under guardians and stewards until the time appointed by the father." God is waiting for his sons to exemplify maturity, and then He will order the guardians to release your wealth at the appointed time.

What does God check in a believer as a sign of maturity before releasing wealth? These four parameters are a starting point.

## RESPONSIBILITY

One quality of maturity is the ability to handle responsibility. As a parent, my joy is to see our children grow in wisdom and stature. When they cook simple meals or do homework and daily chores without supervision, it shows growth and increases my confidence to add more responsibilities.

When a person is responsible with their current wealth, God releases more wealth and responsibility to him or her. Do you pay your tithe? Do you give alms to the needy? Is the money in your hands a blessing to other believers?

How you spend your money speaks on your level of responsibility.

## ABILITY TO SHARE

Human beings are innately selfish. We must teach our children to share if they are to learn kindness and sharing. For God to release money into our hands, He checks on our ability to share. Your ability to share is a sign of maturity. The amount of money you handle is directly proportional to your ability to give.

The more you give, the more God trusts you with more. To increase your receiving capacity, increase your giving capacity.

## ABILITY TO WORSHIP

*God is spirit, and those who worship him must worship in spirit and truth* (John 4:24). God transfers wealth to individuals who have passed the test of worship. When one freely worships God with what He has given, it means they are ready for wealth transfer. "All this I will give you," the devil said to Jesus after showing Him the kingdoms of the world, "if you will bow down and worship me." (Matthew 4:9). Worship involves sacrifice. A worshiper must be willing to give God priority and pre-eminence over the wealth He trusts them with. When this happens, God transfers more. Our worship should belong to God alone not the wealth He has given to us.

## ABILITY TO DO WARFARE

*A good person leaves an inheritance to his grandchildren, but the wealth of the wicked is reserved for the righteous* (Proverbs 13:22, ISV).

If the wealth God has for us is with our enemies, then every child of God must learn how to fight. *All those who were in distress or in debt or discontented gathered around him, and he became their commander. About four hundred men were with him* (1 Samuel 22:2). At this time, David had no money to offer as he was hiding from King Saul. David took them to war. *Once again David inquired of the Lord, and the Lord answered him, "Go down to Keilah, for I am going to give the Philistines into your hand"…David fought the Philistines and carried off their livestock* (1 Samuel 23:4-5). Eventually, David and his men became wealthy as they continued to conquer the land as per God's instruction. The ability to do warfare is a key sign of maturity and readiness for wealth transfer.

Believers must remember that *the weapons of our warfare are not carnal but mighty in God for pulling down strongholds…* (2 Corinthians 10:4, NKJV). This means, the warfare we do for our wealth must be in accordance to the prophetic word (1 Timothy 1:18). Before a believer prospers physically, they must first prosper spiritually. In the matters of wealth transfer, maturity supersedes spirituality.

# PRINCIPLES

# CHAPTER THREE

# THE PRAYER OF JABEZ

*Jabez cried out to the God of Israel, "Oh, that you would bless me and enlarge my territory! Let your hand be with me, and keep me from harm so that I will be free from pain." And God granted his request.*
(1 Chronicles 4:10)

After Jabez realized the cause of his pain, he did not blame his mother, who probably was long dead. He prayed to God. People live in pain because they are too bitter to pray. Prayer is important; but not just prayer—targeted prayer. You must know what you are telling God. Don't just fumble your prayer with no direction.

As a new Christian, I spent a lot of time praying but saw no results. I complained to God because I had spent a lot of time in His presence, yet I did not get the results I expected. God answered me in a very simple and practical way. He told me to record my prayer, which I did. Then God asked me to consider if I were the one listening to the prayers and answering them, what my answers would be. It was shocking: after an hour of listening to the recording, I realized I had rambled on and not made a single request to God.

For prayer to be effective, it must be specific and prayed in understanding.

The prayer of Jabez is a good example of a targeted prayer. It has five parts.

## BLESS ME

*The blessing of God maketh rich and addeth no sorrow* (Proverbs 10:22).

Jabez realized that honor without the blessing of God is futile. If you are blessed, you cannot be cursed. When Balak the king of Moab saw how powerful the Israelites were, and how they defeated the people they found on their way, he called Balaam to curse the Israelites for him. When Balaam tried to curse them, he failed. He ended up blessing them instead (Numbers 23).

The blessings of God must not be taken casually. God instructed the priest to bless his people saying, "You shall bless my people saying, the Lord bless you…" (Numbers 6:23). The reason we need the blessing of God is to avert evil and invoke spiritual blessings with the understanding that those God blesses no one can curse.

## ENLARGE MY TERRITORY

God wants to enlarge you so that you can have a voice. You also receive power to say no to evil (Matthew 4:8). When the devil tempted Jesus with possessions, Jesus said no, reiterating that God alone is to be worshipped and served. All Jesus had to do was bow down and worship the devil, and He would get all the kingdoms of the world and their glory. Many are enticed by the promise of quick wealth and fall because of greed; others are victims of the same because of poverty.

As God blessed Abraham, he released enlargement. "I will surely bless you and make your descendants as numerous as the stars in the sky and as the sand on the seashore. Your descendants will take possession of the cities of their enemies" (Genesis 22:17).

Some people have been despised and have gone through perpetual pain because of the size of their territories. This is what enlargement will do for you:

## ENLARGEMENT GIVES YOU AUTHORITY

you can speak on a matter without fear of public opinion because your opinion carries influence. The enlargement of the Israelites was a threat to their enemies. Pharaoh spoke to his people in alarm, "They are way too many of these Israelites for us to handle" (Exodus 1:9, MSG).

## ENLARGEMENT BREAKS THE YOKER

*"...the yoke will be broken because you have grown so fat" (Isaiah 10:27b).* Enlargement automatically breaks some yokes in your life. When I did not have daily fare and food, I spent my prayer time asking for these things, but when God enlarged my territory, these things I give thanks for daily provision and my prayer list has totally changed. Some battles are only won through enlargement.

## ENLARGEMENT IS A PROOF THAT GOD IS ON YOUR SIDE

The blessing of the LORD makes *one* rich, and He adds no sorrow with it (Proverbs 10:22, NKJV). Riches are seen in enlargement. Job's wealth was not spiritual; it was physical. The Philistine king chased Isaac away but when he was enlarged, he sought for him. *"Isaac asked them, 'Why have you come to me, since you were hostile to me and sent me away?' They answered, "we saw clearly that the Lord was with you"* (Genesis 26:27-28). Enlargement means results. People can argue about your impact until they see results.

**ENLARGEMET DEALS WITH DISDAIN**

"Now there was found in it a poor wise man, and he by his wisdom delivered the city. Yet no one remembered that same poor man." (Ecclesiastes 9:15)

If one is poor, no matter how wise they could be; they will always be despised. This is because enlargement is one proof of God's favour and attention towards you. When it happens, those who disdained or despised you become your cheering squad. "Many rebuked him and told him to be quiet, but he shouted all the more, "Son of David, have mercy on me!" Jesus stopped and said, "Call him." So they called to the blind man, "Cheer up! On your feet! He's calling you" (Mark 10:48-49).

When your territory has been enlarged, some injustices are automatically dealt with. May God enlarge your territory for His glory.

## LET YOUR HAND BE WITH ME

This is a good point to remember when we pray. Jabez asked God to hold his hand. This has to do with fellowship. The reason people lose their breakthrough as soon as they get it is because they let go of God's hand. They want the blessings and not the "Blesser". Remember the story of the prodigal son who left his father as soon as he got his property? Whatever God gives, He protects.

Many people tend to seek God more in prayer and fasting when they are in problems. As soon as their problems are solved, they forget the God who provided and answered their prayers. They will remember God when they need another miracle. During the post-election violence of 2007 in Kenya, churches were filled to capacity and many people gave their lives to Jesus. When the matter settled, many went back to their normal lifestyle forgetting their fervent prayers and return to God.

Jabez must have known prosperity has enemies, for the number of enemies increase as your territory increases. I tell my sons that an empty house does not need a padlock. I saw this firsthand growing up: we never had a padlock on our doors. As an adult visiting one holiday, I was shocked to find there were padlocks on every door. "Were thieves born after we left the village," I asked my father. "In your time, there was nothing to protect," he responded.

The phrase "let your hand be with me" teaches me I should seek to get close to God and feel the warmth of His hand on me. As you rise and as your territories enlarge, and your enemies increase, it becomes necessary to keep your relationship with God tight, or you risk losing everything from a single attack by the enemy.

Though Job was very wealthy, he had a very tight relationship with God—so tight that God was proud of him. When God asked Satan whether he had taken notice of Job, the friend of God, Satan complained that He had protected Job and all his wealth. It seems to me that Satan had tried to touch the prosperity of Job but couldn't because God was in the picture. If you will keep your relationship with God right and tight, God will protect whatever He blesses you with. The richer you become or the more prosperous you get, the tighter you need God to hold your hand.

## KEEP ME FROM HARM

The thief, who is the devil, comes only to steal and kill and destroy (John 10:10a); this is his vision and his mission statement. Since the devil is not changing his behavior or commitment, it is important for us to know that he is always after causing harm, hence the reason to pray against it. The devil is happy when he steals your life, your children, your health, your joy, your peace, your family—but the Son of God came that you may have life (John 10:10b).

Every believer should pray for protection. Before Jesus ascended to heaven, He asked God to keep his disciples safe. *My prayer is not that you take them out of this world but that you protect them from the evil one* (John 17:15).

## HONOR AND PAIN

> *Jabez was more honorable than his brothers. His mother had named him Jabez saying, 'I gave birth to him in pain'"* (1 Chronicles 4:9).

I will use Jabez to describe people who look like they are doing well in every way but they have a thorn in the flesh that makes them cry in their closets. They are honored wherever they go, yet they are sad in their hearts. People admire their lives but they really are putting up a facade. They get a job and someone is planted in their place of work to inflict pain on them. These people may be married to a good-looking person but nothing good comes out of that marriage. They may be victims of perennial abuse but cannot ask for help because they must protect their image.

Do you know people who work hard and smart yet are forever in pain? They build beautiful houses only for intruders to invade them. They cook food but other people eat it instead. They are well educated but cannot secure gainful employment.

Jabez researched the cause of his pain and traced it to the day and the time of his birth. He realized that his mother called him 'pain' because she had been through a lot of pain during childbirth. Some things that inflict pain in people's lives can be traced to their time of birth when the baby is vulnerable and at the mercy of the attendants. The mother at this point is a key person in shaping the child's destiny.

At the time of naming a child, it is important for parents to know that names have meaning. Jabez was called "pain" and pain followed him. Though he was successful enough to receive honor, pain still followed him. Some people go through pain and struggle all the time but they have never known how to pray or what to do. The most powerful thing that God gave Jesus was the NAME above all names. It is this name that we can call upon to receive our salvation, healing, and deliverance.

# CHAPTER FOUR

# DEVELOP FINANCIAL INTEGRITY

Integrity is not a gift, but a product of hard work and strict discipline. Imagine talking to someone about his integrity issues, and the very next day, he says to you he is now a person of integrity because he prayed for integrity the whole night, and God gave it to him. One gains integrity, financial integrity included, by daily practice; it just does not fall upon you. Integrity is not a reserve for a chosen few; anyone can work to get it. However, discipline is necessary, or you risk losing your integrity.

"The man of integrity walks securely, but he who takes crooked paths will be found out" (Proverbs 10:9). Financial integrity has to do with being accountable and truthful. This means not living a lie; it is knowing your true financial status and not trying to portray to others a financial position that you are not. A person of integrity is always secure in his deals and his way. I am not writing this because I am perfect; I work on my integrity daily. When I turned 40, a friend called to wish me a happy birthday and asked, "What's your plan now that you have come to the 4th floor?" My response was I would continue to work at being a man of integrity, whose words and promises are as good as a banker's check.

A person who practices integrity wins people's trust. Zig Ziglar in *The Life Lifters* states: "Without character there is no trust. Successful people are men and women of integrity. They do the right things. They trust themselves and in turn are trusted. With integrity, they have nothing to fear, for there is nothing to hide". Every person believing God to break financial strongholds must, therefore, uphold integrity.

Prophet Samuel, at the end of his leadership tenure, asked the Israelites questions no leader would ask unless they have walked in integrity. "Whose ox have I taken? Whose donkey have I taken? Whom have I cheated? Whom have I oppressed? From whose hand have I accepted a bribe to make me shut my eyes? If I have done any of these things, I will make it right." "You have not cheated or oppressed us," they replied. "You have not taken anything from anyone's hand" (1 Samuel 12:3-4).

The following are different parameters you can use to check your financial integrity.

## LIVE WITHIN YOUR MEANS

Society has a way of constantly demanding more of our money and us. We feel the need to have trendier clothes, smarter phones, and bigger houses in posh neighborhoods, all to please the Jones'.

Society may demand that you drive a certain type of car, live in a certain neighborhood, or even take your children to a certain school as a measure of your financial success. However, it is important to take stock and count the cost of every financial decision. For instance, before you buy your next big purchase, you must think through and answer why you want to acquire it. Is it because you need it or to satisfy your ego? Is the item a necessity or a luxury? And can you afford it? And is it the right time to make the purchase. If it is a car, for example, perhaps you are a student and buying a car may not be a priority. A car will require fuel, insurance, general maintenance, and many other costs. You might need to relocate if you buy a car, for security, space or prestige. All these issues, if not properly considered, can make you lose your financial integrity in the long run.

You should not interpret living within your financial ability as a lack of faith. There are people who feel I live below my status and that I should 'upgrade' to a different neighborhood or a showroom vehicle. The truth is, I live in line with 1 Timothy 6:6, "But godliness with contentment is great gain". Life has no rehearsal, so live it as truthfully as you can.

## MY PRAYER FOR YOU

*May you learn to be content in every situation, whether living in plenty or in want. May you know that God loves you and is concerned about your needs. May He give you the courage to go through seasons of lack and to be generous in times of abundance.*

*Amen.*

## MAKE AN HONEST LIVING

When you know what you own was rightfully acquired, you have no reason to fear or look over your shoulders. One of the reasons why people lack financial integrity is because they own things obtained through crooked means. Wealth acquired in this manner always attracts some level of guilt.

People accused Zacchaeus of acquiring wealth through crooked means, and were even offended that Jesus was associating with him. But when Zacchaeus met Jesus, he pledged to pay back four times all that he had taken from people, and to give half of his possessions to the poor (Luke 19:7-9). I am sure this action gave Zacchaeus freedom and a clean start towards living in financial integrity.

The person who ekes his living, earning his own money is different from one who waits for donations. The test of integrity is more apparent when accounting for money given by people for a specific purpose. If you are fond of looking for free money, you can end up compromising your integrity.

Robert Greene, in *The 48 Laws of Power*, encourages us to despise free lunch. He says, when you pay your own way, you stay free from indebtedness; for free offers are rarely without a hidden agenda. That hidden obligation has been used to bring many leaders down by compromising their financial integrity.

Wealth gained through crooked means will require crooked ways to maintain it. "Dishonest money dwindles away, but he who gathers money little by little makes it grow" (Proverbs 13:11).

## Choose your company wisely

"Bad company corrupts good character" (1 Corinthians 15:33).

Some people have no financial integrity because of the company they keep. If you closely walk and relate with people who don't value financial integrity, even if you value it yourself, you will soon lose it. If one walks with the wise he becomes wise (Proverbs 13:20). In the same way, if one walks with people of integrity he will catch the virtue.

In the first verse of the first Psalm, the psalmist warns against keeping the wrong company and encourages us to meditate on the Law of the Lord. It corroborates the saying, "show me your friends and I will tell your character". The Bible has great examples of men of integrity we can emulate. Choose to keep company with people who value integrity.

Additionally, choose the company of people who can check on your financial growth. You need friends who can tell you to slow down if they notice some wrong financial appetites; friends who can help you define success in a godly way and not out of covetousness.

I once noticed a friend acquire property at a very high rate, not commensurate with his known income streams. When I enquired about his alternative source of income, he beat around the bush and never quite gave me a straightforward answer. Within a short time, he had bought land and built a mansion in a posh neighborhood. However, it did not take long before he lost all he had gathered to banks and loan sharks. He later confessed entering a peer association where competition for material possessions was rife. The more properties one had, the more successful they were perceived to be, so he kept borrowing to remain on top.

The company you keep ought to cheer you on, but also slow you down sometimes. Success is like beauty; it is defined according to the eyes of the beholder. Success can also be like a mirage; it may give the appearance of something real only to disappear when one gets closer. Learn to tell the difference.

# Keep Your Financial Promises

People who make financial promises and never fulfill them have no financial integrity. Every time you make a financial promise to God or to a person, you must work to fulfill it. God honors those who make and fulfill their promises. He also holds you accountable for every promise and vow you make to Him.

Jacob is a good example of a man who made a vow to God and fulfilled it. As Jacob was running away from his brother Esau, he spent his night in Bethel and there he told God, "If God will be with me and will watch over me on this journey I am taking and will give me food and clothes to wear so that I return safely to my father's house… all that you give me, I will give you a tenth" (Genesis 28:20-22).

After God prospered him, he spoke to him referring to the promise Jacob had made. God told him, "… I am the God of Bethel…where you made a vow to me…" (Genesis 32:12).

These verses show that God takes our financial vows or promises seriously. He does not forget when we make promises to Him and holds us accountable for the vows and promises we make, just as He holds those who don't pay their workers their dues. "Pay them their wages each day before sunset, because they are poor and are counting on it. Otherwise they may cry to the Lord against you, and you will be guilty of sin" (Deuteronomy 24:15).

Many people have failed financially because they make vows but fail to fulfill them.

Some people come to me for help and tell me they have been going through financial difficulties. I know that it can be nor- mal to go through a financial difficulty sometimes, but when the case is persistent, I dig in to find out whether they have been fulfilling their financial vows or promises. It is important to go through your financial life and see whether you have made a financial vow to God or people and have not honored it. If so, seek to honor it. Otherwise it can work against your financial breakthrough.

A minister friend received an invitation to preach at a church raising money to build a sanctuary. They were hoping to raise $50,000. In his excitement, he promised to pay 10% of the amount. After the service, he wrote a check for $500, believing that to be the 10% he had pledged. His wife, on seeing the amount he had written, reminded him that he still had $4,500 to pay. The man ended up paying the whole $5,000 although he hadn't really planned to give that much. He had to do it for the purpose of keeping the financial promise he had made in front of the congregation.

Failure to keep your financial promises, however small they may be, ends up affecting your financial integrity. It is always prudent to think before you utter a vow so you make promises you will be able to fulfill.

## PAY YOUR DEBTS

The ability to pay what you owe is a sign of financial integrity. It is not the will of God that we live in debt. Some debts are so enslaving they take away one's peace or joy for life. Some people get into debt having already made up their minds not to pay up. If you want to be a person of integrity, then you must convince your mind that it is not good to live in debt. Paying up the debt that you committed to pay is a show of integrity.

God instructed the Israelites to free each other from debts after every seven years. "At the end of every seven years you must cancel debts… Every creditor shall cancel any loan they have made to a fellow Israelite" (Deuteronomy 15:1-3). God wishes that we live a debt-free life but because of our human limitations, and sometimes our hearts' desires, we find ourselves in debt. Debt takes away your authority. The Bible says that a borrower is a slave to the lender (Proverbs 22:7).

As much as possible, work to live a debt-free life. However, I don't want to condemn anyone for being in debt. Not all debts are bad. Robert Kiyosaki, in *Cashflow Quadrant*, says, "Every time you owe someone money, you become an employee of their money. If you take out a 30-year loan, you've become a 30-year employee, and they do not give you a gold watch when the debt is retired…good debt is debt that someone else paid for you and bad debt is what you paid for with your own sweat and blood." That is why, Robert says he loves rental properties, "because the bank gives you a loan to build them, but your tenants pay for it". As far as Robert is concerned, any debt you can make others pay for is debt you can get into. I couldn't agree more. If you find yourself in debt that is not 'good', below are simple ways you can begin to deal with your debt.

## PRAY TO GOD FOR HELP

Before you get into any major debt, pray. Many people jump into debt without praying to God and then remember Him when things go wrong. We ought to ask God in prayer, whether it is okay to get into a certain debt. I do not mean informing God that you are getting into debt, but the prayer that seeks to know God's will over the matter. This is the kind of prayer where one has to ask and wait on God for the answer. If you are married, it is important to involve your spouse so you can pray over the matter together.

If you get stuck and cannot pay up a debt you had involved God initially, then you should go back to the same God for further direction. Running away from your creditors is not the solution. Pray to God for help. In the Lord's Prayer, we ask God to forgive us our debts as we forgive others. It is possible for a debtor to suffer when perhaps a creditor is seeking to forgive them. Our God is a debt-cancelling

God. He instructed the Israelites to forgive or cancel any debts owed by their fellow Israelites in the year of jubilee.

In prayer, you receive a strategy from God that enables you to come out of your debt. After receiving the strategy, you must then take action. The first action is a mindset change: you need to convince yourself that paying off your debt is possible and you will not give in to despair. If cancellation of your debt is in any other way other than paying it back, let the miracle find you paying according to your plan, so you are not relying on wishful thinking.

Start by paying the smallest debt first. According to a Spanish proverb, *Debts are like children: the smaller they are the more noise they make.* Owing little money can also be embarrassing. Imagine everyone in the neighborhood where you live knows you don't pay for your milk and eggs. Paying off the smallest amounts of debt first also creates a small win that encourages the debtor to face bigger debts.

After paying off the smallest debts, deal with the sensitive ones next to avoid more serious repercussions. Rent arrears or shylock loans can be very sensitive because of high interest rates, the threat of auctioneers or the risk of eviction or being homeless in the case of rent arrears.

Do not wait until you have enough to clear your debts at once. Don't just plan how you will pay your debt; begin paying! Give yourself a deadline that will keep you on your toes. Clear your debts as money comes and do not wait for the point called 'enough'; that point never arrives.

*A hundred wagonloads of thoughts will not pay a single ounce of debt*
Italian proverb.

## HAVE AN ACCOUNTABILITY PARTNER

Some debts never get paid up because only the debtor and creditor know them. If you owe someone money, let a friend know of your plan to pay for accountability purposes. Update them regularly on your progress. Give your accountability partner the details of your deadlines and your expected sources of income that you intend to use to clear your debt. This accountability partner should be able to follow you up and check or measure your progress using the parameters you give them. The Bible encourages us to confess our sins one to another (James 5:16); I also encourage us to confess our debts one to another. An African proverb puts it this way: *If you hide the fire from me, you will not hide the smoke.* Confiding in a friend or an accountability partner gives some inner peace, even as one works at repaying what they owe.

## DO NOT CELEBRATE BEING IN DEBT

> *I'm in debt. I am a true American.*
> Balki Bartokomous

Many people, instead of realizing the importance of paying up their debts, look for phrases to encourage themselves in their situation.

I once fell into this trap. My wife showed concern over a debt I owed whose repayments just never seemed to end. When she asked me about my plans, I brushed her off: saying that even America owes China some money.

I had a wrong attitude, which did not help my cause to be debt-free. It is not good to celebrate being in debt; it only attracts another of its kind. In other words, it becomes a lifestyle.

If you don't feel guilty when in debt or don't strive to pay up, then most likely you are celebrating being in it.

In a later chapter, I will discuss some of the dangers of not carefully managing debt.

# CHAPTER FIVE

# PRINCIPLES OF ADMINISTERING GOD'S RESOURCES

God has no problem releasing resources to you. It is His joy and delight to give to His children their inheritance. One parameter God uses to see whether His children are ready for resources is maturity.

I suppose that by now you believe that God responds to prayers. However, God is very caring and concerned about His children, yet some answers to prayer are based on the believer's maturity. Knowing how to count money is not proof that one can handle money. You require maturity to properly handle money. God in his wisdom does not release money to you if they are still underage. Remember that story of the prodigal son (Luke 15:11-32). Though he was of age he was not ready to handle money. As soon as he received his share of the estate, he sold it and soon became a pauper. *What I am saying is that as long as an heir is underage, he is no different from a slave, although he owns the whole estate. The heir is subject to guardians and trustees until the time set by his father. So it is also, when we were underage, we were in slavery under the elemental spiritual forces of the world* (Galatians 4:1-3).

No matter how much a child prays, pleads and begs or how much the father loves the child, as long as the child is not 18 (or 16 in some countries), the father cannot give that child a car to drive. No matter how spiritual one becomes, if they do not mature up, they will not receive some resources from God, because in the matters of ownership, maturity supersedes spirituality.

Once we have received from God, then we are expected to be good stewards of His resources. We are good stewards if we observe these principles:

## LIVE BY FAITH BUT WORK WITHIN OUR BUDGET

A Christian cannot live by sight. There are so many things God has called us to do that are achieved only by faith. If a vision is of God then it will always demand beyond my pocket's ability. This means that I must depend on the God of the vision for my provision. Similarly, God has given me a mind to think. My mind tells me that I need to work within my budget. Faith is not foolishness nor is it abstract. Faith is real and tangible. This is why the Bible calls it the "substance" of things not seen (Hebrews 11:1). Faith should not be confused for wishful thoughts, which have lead many to debt and out of God's will.

Faith and works go together according to James 2:14-26.

## IF YOU CANNOT AFFORD IT, IT IS NOT A GOOD DEAL

An item is only a good deal if you have the money to pay for it. In my language (Chuka) we say, "Commenting on how fat a bull is does not mean slaughter it". The fact that a deal is good does not mean you should go for it. There were many beautiful girls when I was looking for a wife but I had to choose just one. It does not mean all others were bad. No! I just needed one. You do not need to spend beyond your means because it was a "once in a lifetime offer". There may be many good deals, but you don't need all of them.

## NO GOLD HAS LEFT THE PLANET EARTH

Many people are always in debt because of instant gratification: the urgency to have it now. I have observed that as long as earth remains, money will remain and buying and selling will never cease. Don't be harassed to buy a certain piece of property because "it will be very expensive later". If you can't afford it now, let it go. No gold is leaving the planet earth. You can buy it later. It may be slightly more expensive then, but more affordable to you at that time. Do not allow yourself to fall for the "buy now while stocks last" marketing strategy. Instead, learn the value of delayed or deferred gratification, and save and plan for your purchases rather than being impulsive.

## BEFORE YOU COMMIT, ASK GOD

Being a good steward means asking the Master how to spend the resources He has entrusted you with. Some things we say we would "die" to have, we don't really need them. Giving God a chance to talk to us before we spend our money can be profitable. God can make you rich by telling you what to go for and what to avoid.

Don't commit yourself to a loan for the sake of having money in your pocket. Research for the cheapest credit if you've got to get into debt. Remember, some commitments are extremely painful once they have been entered into. There are good things out there that you do not need. The ability to say "no" or to wait is the key to breaking financial limitations. Go for delayed satisfaction rather than instant gratification.

## ALTHOUGH YOU CAN AFFORD IT, DOESN'T MEAN YOU OUGHT TO BUY IT

There are many things that I can afford, yet I do not need. Buying what one does not need can easily lead to debt. One way to come out of debt is to dispose off your excesses (things you have but don't necessarily need). It is a good discipline to constantly ask God whether you should purchase a thing.

## INCREASED INCOME DOES NOT NECESSARILY MEAN "SPEND MORE"

I know a man in his twenties who married a second wife. When I asked him why, he told me he had had a salary increment, and it had proved hard for his first wife to utilize all the income. This seemed like a joke, but I went away thinking how many people I know who have lifestyle changes because of additional income.

You must handle any financial increment with thanksgiving to God and follow God's direction on what to do with the surplus. When you have an increment in your income, it would be prudent to remain in the same house, drive the same car, and eat in the same star hotel for some time so you can find maintain sobriety. Hurrying to spend will lead to impulse buying and over-commitment, which can lead to debt despite the extra income. I was at prayer center one time asking God to provide $1000 so I could pay off a certain debt. In the same center, there was a man asking God how he can bless others with his $10,000 surplus.

His prayer reminded me the importance of going back to God for direction, not just when in lack, but in increase too.

## DON'T DWELL ON THE YESTER PAIN

Life has ups and downs. People go through profits and losses. No wonder the Bible encourages us to diversify. *Give portions to seven, yes to eight, for you do not know what disaster will come upon the land* (Ecclesiastes 11:2). People who sit down to mourn their past mistakes hardly break their financial strongholds. Risk-takers use past pain or loss as a strategy for their next move. Don't dwell on yester pain; learn to forgive and move on. There are many entrepreneurs whose businesses failed, yet because they did not give up but worked hard, they are now very successful.

You might ask, "Have you ever burnt your fingers?" My answer is, "Of course, yes!" I choose to count my losses as school fees. Those who have never gone through pain in the course of trying out different ventures are those who have done nothing yet. Financial breakthrough may be gradual. You might not succeed the very first time you undertake a venture, but I urge you not to live on the pain and loss. Learn from your mistakes and move on.

# CHAPTER SIX

# THE HARVEST MENTALITY

No person can break the spirit of poverty without a harvest mentality. Many preachers teach about sowing, and there is nothing wrong with that, but Jesus brought the aspect of harvest. *The harvest is plentiful but the workers are few. Ask the Lord of the harvest, therefore, to send out workers into his harvest field"* (Matthew 9:37-38). My interpretation is that laborers could be looked at as being few in number or in mentality.

It is important to note that having a harvest mentality is not equal to begging. Begging is a bad spirit that makes people poor and keeps them enslaved. I do not celebrate when developing countries are given grants by the developed countries. I know very well that the more one receives handouts, the more they become dependent on the donor, and in reality, the poorer they become. No person becomes rich through begging; if anything, they graduate into higher levels of begging.

I once engaged in a conversation with a beggar in the street. Upon inquiring how much he made per day, I gave him more money than he had quoted as his daily take home. I expected him to pack and leave, having met his target for the day. Instead, he pretended to leave, and once I was out of sight, returned to his begging position. Since I was meeting a friend near that locality, my friend decided to ask the beggar the same question I had asked. It was no surprise when the beggar quoted a higher amount as his daily take-home than he had originally given to me.

Harvesting is work. People labor to plant and they must also labor to harvest.

As a young man, I served as a caretaker in our church compound. One morning, I woke up bitter because I felt. God was not giving me the money I needed to meet my needs. Then I heard an inner voice tell me to clean every car that came into our church compound that day. Now, I must say that only my pastor's car was a "regular", but that particular day, God brought more than six vehicles to the compound and I cleaned them with joy. I remember how excited the owners were when they found their cars cleaned. Each one reached for their wallets to appreciate me with money, but I quickly declined, saying, I was not doing the job to be paid. They were all willing to give me some money as a token of appreciation, but according to me, I never deserved pay from man, only God. When evening came, I was the same broke boy. I complained to God in prayer and this is what He said, "I gave you money but you refused." Immediately the car owners came to mind and I could hear myself saying, "Thank you sir, I never did this for pay." My problem was simple; I did not have a harvest mentality. People with a harvest mentality, have the following characteristics:

## THEY SEE AND SEIZE OPPORTUNITIES

*...the race is not to the swift or the battle to the strong, nor does food come to the wise or wealth to the brilliant or favour to the learned; but time and chance happens to them all* (Ecclesiastes 9:11).

God gives opportunities to every human being, but not every human being sees or seizes them. Opportunities are like revolving doors—they keep circling. It is up to you to time your turn and enter. This is what I call seizing the opportunity. God will always revolve chances or opportunities for you, and it is up to you to master the art of seizing your opportunity.

Some people break financial limits faster than others because of their ability to identify and seize the opportunities availed to them.

To be able to see opportunities, one must see beyond the "now". Some opportunities come in incubators; they will require you to see the future in them rather than the present, and to have patience to see it come to fruition.

My wife once received some money and thought investing in land would be a prudent way to make use of the cash. She went ahead and looked for land, and very excitedly took me to see it. The deal was good—less than $300 for about three acres. When I saw the land, I despised it because it was rocky. I discouraged my wife from buying, and being an obedient wife, she did not buy the land. A few years later, something special happened in the location where the land was, and the land prices shot up in an unbelievable way. The same piece of land was now selling for $300,000. I almost could not forgive myself, even though my wife had forgiven me for "misleading" her. She had seen an opportunity with a futurist eye. I, on the other hand, had missed the opportunity because I relied on present appearance, and only saw rocks.

## THEY TURN OPPORTUNITIES INTO RESOURCES

A story is told of Christians who went for a mission in a poor country. People gave their lives to Jesus and the mission was successful. Upon their return, they moved the whole church to tears as they explained the poverty in that nation. They shared how the people in that country had no food and no shoes.

As they gave their report, a man visiting the church for the first time was taking notes. He later went and found out the exact place where the team had ministered. A few days later, he bought shoes and clothes that he thought would be affordable to the brethren in that poor nation and shipped them for sale. Within a short time, this visitor was a millionaire. He had seized a business opportunity of providing affordable clothing to people who didn't have money to buy expensive ones.

In the church today, many congregants have many opportunities but have never turned them into resources. If you want to know I am right, go to church and listen as people pray in the spirit, and give testimonies of the great revelations they receive from God. You can get lots of free information that you can turn into business ideas that can make you rich.

I tell my church members that revelation is given to elevate and so it is better to work at getting an elevation from a revelation than to share the revelation as proof that one is connected with God.

Imagine this scenario; there is no rain in the land. Responding to the word of God, pastors call for a prayer, fasting, and repentance meeting. Then God pours the rain upon the earth. The holy people who called for the rain now change from praying for the rain to thanking God for the rain, but do not plant their fields. Meanwhile, an atheist who never prayed, fasted, or repented, who does not even believe there is a God in heaven, plants his maize and beans in due season. Of the two, who do you think is worthy of the harvest? No matter how ungodly the atheist is, as long as he seized the opportunity (rain) and turned it into a resource (planted/sowed), he will enjoy the harvest, while the holy people who prayed and fasted for the rain go hungry.

Further, the atheist will be very rich because he will enjoy the monopoly of selling his farm produce to the holy believers who prayed for the rains but never planted.

May you never miss your opportunity!

It is important to note here that peoples' problems could be the opportunities you need to seize and turn into resources. The jobless people around you could be your employees if only you changed your perception. If you see them as a bother, you miss the point. But if you can create jobs for them, then you will prosper. No human being was created empty and without purpose by God. We are each loaded with something within us and created for a purpose.

## THEY PRAY AND DEPEND ON GOD'S FAVOUR

Favour is a currency every believer must have. Queen Esther asked Mordecai to pray and fast with her so she could get favour with the king, her husband. God answered Esther's prayer. This means that one can pray for favour from God. My wife and I use this slogan every time we need to get something done and seem not to have money: "use favour until the money comes".

Ruth believed God for favour as she went out to harvest. *Let me go to the fields and pick up the leftover grain behind anyone in whose eyes I find favour* (Ruth 2:2). Without God's favour, it is very difficult to break the spirit of poverty. I know people who have labored, worked both smart and hard, and lacked favour; and so they never prospered.

One such person shared with me his pain in life. He had done everything a person can do to break poverty, but was still unable to make ends meet and, as it were, was living from hand to mouth.

Then I heard a whisper: "favour". I asked God to favour him and he left. I told him to go back and do the things he had tried to do before. It didn't take long before he returned to testify what God had done for him.

## MY PRAYER FOR YOU

*May God favour you in whatever you put your hands to do. May favour distinguish and lift you to higher heights. Like Ruth was favoured in a foreign land, may God favour you in foreign circumstances, nations, and careers. Like Nehemiah, may you find favour with kings and those in authority. May that favour come with supplies for the vision God has given you.*

*Amen.*

# PRACTICAL APPLICATION

# CHAPTER SEVEN

# THE POWER OF GIVING

*Giving is more than a responsibility—it is a privilege;
more than an act of obedience—it is evidence of our faith.*
William Arthur Ward, American educator

Two things describe God's actions towards humanity: love and giving. *For God so loved the world that he gave his only begotten son...* (John 3:16). In the same way, there are two things that show whether a person will prosper or not: their love for God and His people, and their giving to both. The reason God blesses people with money is so they can continue representing Him on earth through giving.

Giving and loving are inseparable, though love is superior to giving. It is possible to give without love, but it is not possible to love without giving. The one universal language the world understands is love, and the one test you must pass as you serve God and humanity is giving. God tested Abraham's love through giving. In Genesis 22, God asked Abraham for the sacrifice of his only son. As soon as Abraham proved he was willing and ready to sacrifice, God blessed him with prosperity. If you have not passed the test of giving, then you have not passed the test of love.

If you are working to break financial strongholds, giving is part of the remedy. Here are other reasons why we should give.

## GOD IS A GIVER

Because God is a giver, we too must give. God asks us to be holy as He is holy. This means He wants us to be like Him. God is an expert giver. He always gives the best. Perhaps the elephants could have given more blood than Jesus did; yet God gave His only Son (Jesus) because of His love for humanity. Likewise, He expects us to be givers.

One day, a friend asked me whether it is a "must" to give tithes and offerings. I told him it is. He also wanted to know whether he should give to God from his gross or net salary. My response to him was, we give so that God can give us more and protect that which remains, according to Malachi 3. Thus we choose what we want God to bless, protect, and increase and give from it. That statement turned out to speak more to me than to my friend. I began to see how God provides for me and that there is nothing I have, which He has not given me, and therefore, I should extravagantly give just as God gives to me.

## GIVING IS INVESTING IN GOD

The best way to keep money in circulation for a long time is through good investments. Every person would want to invest in a secure avenue with a guarantee of good return. By giving, we invest in God and are sure of security and good return. "Do not store up your treasures on earth, where moth and rust destroy and where thieves break in and steal. But store up your treasures in heaven, where moth and rust do not destroy, and where thieves do not break in and steal…" (Matthew 6:19-20). The best place to invest is in God, through people.

Robert Strand shares this story in his book, *Before the Offering is Received*:

"A Methodist layman gave $100,000 to build a college in Liberia in the early 1920s. By the 1940s, the college was growing and meeting the educational and the spiritual needs of many young Africans. On the anniversary of the college's founding, the administration decided it was time to make a formal thank you to the original benefactor.

"It took months for the General Board of missions to track down that layman. He had lost everything in the crash of 1929 and was living in a very humble home on the south side of Chicago. Twice he refused the invitation but finally agreed to go. At their insistence, they flew him to Africa for the gala celebration.

As he looked over the smiling faces of the young students and campus, with tears in his eyes he whispered to the president of the college, 'The only thing I have kept is what I gave away.'"

This is the power of giving and a demonstration of the safety of investing in God. Besides, we will carry nothing from earth except what we send ahead of us when we are alive. Invest for the future now through giving.

## GIVING HAS A VOICE

Giving speaks on your behalf before God. There are places you may not go to and offices you may not have access to, but a gift can enter and speak on your behalf.

A centurion had a sick servant and needed Jesus to heal him. For whatever reason, he could not access Jesus, so the centurion sent the Jewish elders to plead with Jesus on his behalf to heal his servant. The elders told Jesus to heal the man because of his giving. "This man deserves to have you do this, because he loves our nation and has built our synagogue" (Luke 7:4-5). One's giving can speak for them. The centurion never spoke to Jesus; the elders spoke on his behalf because he had given to the building of the synagogue.

Givers keep speaking even when they are long dead. I have realized that when I preach, people forget some of my sermons, but they hardly forget my acts of giving. One day, I brought enough bananas for all my church members from my up-country farm. "You may forget my sermon, but I know you will not forget my bananas," I joked. Many years later, at an event, a total stranger walked up to me saying, "Indeed I forgot your sermon, but I have never forgotten your bananas".

Giving is a voice that does not die with a person. I agree with Robert Greene's view in *48 Laws of Power*, that generosity is a sign of power. Sometimes I feel that something went wrong with us Africans. Maybe we silenced our voice when we stopped giving and opened our hands to receive. I attended a church service where the usher collecting the offering by-passed me because they thought I had nothing to give. In another church, someone refunded the money they saw me drop in the offering basket because they thought that as an African, I didn't have anything to give. This usher felt that the little I had should be spared for my use in Africa. Thank God for the knowledge of His word. I knew that nobody prospers through gathering but scattering.

As I preached in church one Sunday, I asked the congregation whether anyone remembered their mother sending them to their neighbor's house to borrow salt and sugar when they were growing up. A large number raised their hands. I then asked whether there were any who were sent to give to the very neighbors, and very few hands were raised. This reiterates that our socialization is amiss. Many people were taught to receive, to borrow, but not to give.

It was not so from the beginning. Africa was a giving continent from ancient times. Even The tabernacle of Moses and the temple of Solomon were built with money from Africa (Egypt). All the resources given to Moses for the building of the tabernacle were given from the wealth the Israelites carried with them from Egypt. The Queen of Sheba from Ethiopia also carried lots of gifts to King Solomon. She did not just go to receive; she had something to give.

## GIVING IS A WARFARE STRATEGY

While we can win every battle through strategy, we win some battles only through giving.

When Jacob was finally going to meet with his brother Esau after taking away his blessing and being away for a long time, he expected Esau to be rough and to fight back. So he divided his property—cows, donkeys, camels, goats, and sheep—into portions and sent them ahead of him with instructions to tell Esau that these were his gifts. All this was in a bid to diffuse and appease Esau's heart (Genesis 33).

*When the Philistines heard that Israel had assembled at Mizpah, the rulers of the Philistines came up to attack them. When the Israelites heard of it, they were afraid because of the Philistines. They said to Samuel, "Do not stop crying out to the Lord our God for us, that he may rescue us from the hand of the Philistines." Then Samuel took a suckling lamb and sacrificed it as a whole burnt offering to the Lord. He cried out to the Lord on Israel's behalf, and the Lord answered him. While Samuel was sacrificing the burnt offering, the Philistines drew near to engage Israel in battle. But that day the Lord thundered with loud thunder against the Philistines and threw them into such a panic that they were routed before the Israelites. The men of Israel rushed out of Mizpah and pursued the Philistines, slaughtering them along the way to a point below Beth Kar (1 Samuel 7: 7-11).*

When we sacrifice, God himself shows up. He showed up for Samuel giving him victory over his enemies. Samuel began by offering a sacrifice to God, then proceeding to pray. Sometimes, if you are facing an unending battle and have spent time in prayer, offering a sacrifice to God concerning the issue, and resting in Him brings a great victory.

There are battles that one wins only by the strength of the weapons one has, but by sacrifice. If you have prayed over a matter and you can't see results, you need to understand that God is not asleep when you pray. Probably God is waiting to see a sacrificial heart. It is important for me to mention here that the God we serve is a God of sacrifice (John 3:16) and He is touched by a heart of sacrifice. Samuel could have prayed for the children of Israel, but he knew that the quickest way of getting the attention of God, and his victory, was through giving. When we pray, God can send an angel (Daniel 10:13) or a human being in response to our requests.

David Oyedepo, in his book *Understanding Financial Prosperity*, shares a testimony of how Oral Roberts received victory from tuberculosis. "When Oral Roberts was on his deathbed as a teenager, he said to his mother, 'I have some tithe in my suit pocket. Help me, go and drop it in church, I don't want to go to heaven owing God.' That is how God healed him."

## GIVING DETERMINES OUR LEVEL OF RECEIVING

No matter how prayerful one is, when it comes to receiving, God releases to people according to their measure of giving and not just their faith; for He is never mocked. Whoever gives coins has the grace to receive coins. By giving, one determines their level of receiving. In other words, one attracts what they give. Remember, it is in the measure that you give, that you shall receive, pressed down, shaken together and running over (Luke 6:38).

You can never break poverty by aggressive begging or borrowing, but aggressive giving can. The level of our giving reveals our level of faith in the One to whom we give, and our expected return.

## GIVING CONFIRMS OUR SALVATION

I once saw a cartoon depicting a man being baptized. His whole body was immersed in the water except for his hand, which was lifted above the water holding up his wallet. The implication being, God had his heart but not his money. You have not really encountered God's touch unless you are willing to let Him touch your finances too.

Zacchaeus, after encountering Jesus, talked of giving his possessions to the poor and paying back those from whom he had stolen. In other words, Zacchaeus confirmed his salvation by his actions. "Jesus said to him, 'Today salvation has come to this house, because this man, too, is a son of Abraham'" (Luke 19:9 ).

Do you remember the story of the rich young man in the Bible? He wanted to know from Jesus the requirements for having eternal life.

> Jesus replied, *"You shall not murder, you shall not commit adultery, you shall not steal, you shall not give false testimony, honor your father and mother, and love your neighbor as yourself." "All these I have kept," the young man said. "What do I still lack?" Jesus answered,"If you want to be perfect, go, sell your possessions and give to the poor, and you will have treasure in heaven. Then come, follow me." When the young man heard this, he went away sad, because he had great wealth* (Matthew 19:18-22).

He qualified in all the things that Jesus mentioned to him except regarding his wealth and riches. These are matters of giving.

## MY PRAYER FOR YOU

*May He who supplies seed to the sower and bread for food, also supply and increase your store of seed and enlarge the harvest of your righteousness. May He make you rich in every way so that you can be generous on every occasion (2 Corinthians 9:10,11). May God remember all your sacrifices and accept all your offerings. May He give you the desire of your heart and make all your plans succeed (Psalm 20:4, 5).*

*Amen.*

# CHAPTER EIGHT

# THE DANGER OF UNMANAGED DEBT

Debt is like fire. If controlled and used well, you will enjoy its warmth and can even use it to cook. The same fire, if it gets out of control, can irreparably destroy a whole neighborhood. Debts can grow to be very dangerous if they are not properly handled. These are the dangers I have seen resulting from unmanaged debt.

## DEBTS CAN DESTROY RELATIONSHIPS AND FAMILIES

Debt is one of the reasons many families have broken up. I mentioned earlier that it is important for a couple to pray and agree before they get into any debt. Sometimes people enter into debt without involving their spouses, for what seems like very genuine reasons like: "The deal was too good to let go" or "You too could not have resisted it" or even "I tried reaching you, but you were *mteja* (out of reach) and I had to make a quick decision."

A friend met with a former colleague who seemed to be doing very well. He told my friend stories of his success, which sparked his interest. The former colleague quickly gave my friend an opportunity to supply goods to a seemingly reputable company. The deal was so good, and having come from a friend and former colleague, he never gave prayer or second thought a chance. He quickly withdrew all the money he had in his account, bought the goods, and supplied them. When his goods were received in the company's office, he was congratulated and offered another tender, this time round, bigger than what his friend had given. He called one of his good friends to borrow additional money, telling him he would repay in two weeks. All this time, unfortunately, his wife was not in the know.

He continued to borrow from other friends and shylocks because he saw this venture as a God-sent opportunity.

When the date was due to pick up his paycheck, he happily went to the office, only to find that the premises were now occupied by a salon and the occupants knew nothing about the previous occupants.

Worried and stressed, the man began to Google to find the whereabouts of the company. He was shocked to learn that the whole deal was a scam. Later, he learned that his former colleague had lost his job many years back and was now a conman. You can now imagine the next step of action. He had used all the money the family had without the knowledge of his wife, and was now deep in debt, owing both friends and financial institutions. To cut the story short, his family is no longer with him, and as for the friends, you can guess.

## DEBT LOWERS SELF-ESTEEM

Debts have a way of lowering one's self-esteem. Depending on the nature of the debt, low self-esteem, and the anxiety that goes with it, unmanaged debt can lead to depression or, worse still, death.

A man in serial debt loses his voice among his peers and becomes hostile to his own people. If a husband loses his self-esteem, his immediate family suffers. In my pastoral ministry, I have handled cases where husbands are extremely brutal to their wives and children. A certain lady told me how her once loving husband had become a monster. After following up on the root cause of the issue, I found out that it all started with a nagging debt that the husband entered into without her knowledge.

## DEBT ENSLAVES THE DEBTOR

*The rich rules over the poor, and the borrower becomes the lender's slave (Proverbs 22:7).*

Debts are enslaving. As long as one is in debt, the mind and actions are in slavery. It is very hard for anyone to have freedom when they owe. It is also hard for someone to defend themselves against their creditors or give opposing views, no matter how oppressive they become. Debts take away the freedom of the borrower.

I have observed that even when a country gets a loan from another country, it is the lender who has influence over decisions made, simply because they are the ones providing the funds. If the donor lends money to build roads, even if the receiving country felt that building schools would be more beneficial to its citizens, it would not do so because the conditions on how to use the money have been stipulated by the lending country.

I believe the reason God called us to be givers, is so that we can have a voice and a mastery of issues. People should also avoid long-term debt because they keep the borrower doing nothing in life other than paying off that debt. Organizations can sometimes use car loans, education loans, mortgages etc., although beneficial, to keep people in the same job even when they no longer find joy and fulfillment.

Some people end up working all their lives without enjoying the work of their hands, just to clear a debt. Remember, debt can be enslaving.

## DEBT LEADS TO ROBBING GOD TO PAY PEOPLE

> *"You are under a curse your whole nation—because you are robbing me. Bring the whole tithe into the storehouse, that there may be food in my house. Test me in this," says the Lord Almighty, "and see if I will not throw open the floodgates of heaven and pour out so much blessing that there will not be room enough to store it"* (Malachi 3:9,10).

Many times when an individual is in debt, they may struggle to pay their tithes and offerings. They become "robbers without violence" in the house of their Father and end up being disobedient children. Some say God will understand that the only money they have in their hands is for their immediate bills, that is, for paying rent and buying food. What this does is that the people of God get caught up in a web of struggle that only gets broken by simply obeying God's command to bring the whole tithe into His storehouse.

There are blessings that accrue to an individual who obeys God's word. Not paying one's tithes and offerings opens the door for the devourer to attack. The same monies that one needed for rent and other urgent utilities end up paying hospital bills or other emergencies that might cost even more than if one had simply tithed.

> *"I will prevent pests from devouring your crops, and the vines in your fields will not drop their fruit before it is ripe," says the Lord Almighty. "Then all the nations will call you blessed, for yours will be a delightful land," says the Lord Almighty* (Malachi 3:11,12).

If we lack obedience in this area, we must pray and trust God to deliver us from this cycle. Tithing is a financial practice or principle that unlocks many other financial benefits for believers. It is the only Scripture in which God allows man to test Him. He commits to protect from the devourer and open the floodgates of His blessings upon the lives of His people because of obedience to His word. May the Lord help you as you commit to excel in this area.

One may ask how much tithe they should give. Is it 10 percent of my gross or net earnings? The question I would throw back at you is, which of the two has God given you? Remember, your very own life is a gift from God, who is the best model of a GREAT giver. People who have received freedom and revelation in this area give far beyond the 10 percent of their gross income because they know that giving shows our gratitude for who the Father is in our lives, and that we return to Him only a small portion of what He has already given to us.

## DEBT CAN RUIN YOUR CREDIBILITY

Once I heard a Kenyan celebrity complain that one of their friends had in the recent past changed drastically. The said friend would no longer pick anyone's calls, and many of their mutual friends had the same complaint. When I listened further, I learned that his business was struggling and he had ended up with many bank loans, which left him with little cash to sustain his lifestyle. As a result, this person was often borrowing from his close friends, who were not aware of what was happening to him. Since he was unable to repay what he owed, it put his relationships in jeopardy. This man had spent a lot of time and money over the years building these relationships, but now they were crumbling fast. His credibility and reputation were at stake because of his debt.

Debts that go unpaid can be a threat to relationships and make people look wicked, like Psalm 37:21 says: "The wicked borrows and does not pay back, But the righteous is gracious and gives." Character is equated to keeping one's word regardless of the cost. The credibility of an individual can be shredded to pieces when they are not able to keep their word at the time they are expected to pay back what they owe.

## DEBT CAN LEAD TO DISHONESTY

Debts can reduce an individual to a serial liar; once you speak one lie, you might need another lie to undo or maintain the first one. This is so especially when one is not able to pay back their debt on time.

There is a man who lied to his wife after she discovered one of their title deeds missing from the house. He denied taking it away and even threatened to kill her if she insisted on asking the same question. What he did not say was that he had entangled himself with money lenders, lost large amounts of money, borrowed from friends, and was selling part of their property to offset what he owed because creditors were on his neck. Since he was also working out of town, he had sold his car without disclosing this to his wife. His desire for quick cash almost put his life and that of his family to ruin, like Proverbs 21:5 says: "The plans of the diligent lead surely to advantage, But everyone who is hasty comes surely to poverty."

If you are honest with yourself about your financial status, you can live a debt-free life. God is able to deliver you from such situations if you are willing and cry out for His help. He is a merciful and gracious Father, *call on me in the day of trouble; I will deliver you, and you will honor me* (Psalm 50:15).

One of the ways to shield yourself from dishonesty is by speaking what you mean and doing what you say. Spend what you have in your hands and not what you have in your heart. What you anticipate to have is what is in your heart.

At the same time, I would encourage you not to make a promise [to pay] to someone based on another promise [to be paid] that you have been given. If the one who gave you a promise does not honor his word, whether for a good or a bad reason, you too will not honor yours. In other words, wait for your promise to materialize and when you have the money in your hands, then you can act.

Dennis Tongoi, in his book *Mixing God With Money*, warns us against spending anticipated income. He says, "Do not spend anticipated income—you place yourself at the mercy of your debtors. If the anticipated income does not come through, you will be left high and dry. You are responsible for your debts and not your debtors." Always remember that the power of a man is in the promises he makes and fulfills, so don't make one based on other peoples' promises.

## DEBTS CAUSE WORRY AND STRESS

Being in debt can be a cause of so much worry and stress, to the extent that some people have committed suicide because they are unable to face consequences like auctioneers coming to claim a luxury car or sell the family house. Some people resort to risky habits like alcoholism, drug abuse or other addictive behavior that leaves their lives in misery. Unpaid debt can fuel destructive habits, broken families, depression, and other negative behavior.

Persons who were once very productive and respectable in the society have their lives degenerate drastically as a result of the trouble that debt brings. Many times, when people get into debt, they get into the cycle of looking for more debt to repay the other debt. This puts them in a fix where more than one creditor is looking for them at any given time, keeping the borrower on the run with no rest.

It is prudent to make wise financial decisions. Those who are married should involve or consult their spouses and walk in unity and agreement in your journey to achieve your financial goals.

Though you may be deep in the belly of debt, keep calling on God. He will come through for you, just like He did for Jonah despite his initial disobedience. "… From the depths of the grave I called for help and you listened to my cry…And the Lord commanded the fish and it vomited Jonah onto dry land" (Jonah 2:2,10).

## MY PRAYER FOR YOU

*May God help you live a debt-free life. I pray that you would receive God's wisdom on how to get out of your current debt situation and recover and restore your resources.*

*Amen.*

# CHAPTER NINE

# LIMITATIONS TO FINANCIAL BREAKTHROUGH

Life is full of limitations that can hinder us from enjoying our financial breakthrough. These limitations come in different forms, as I will explain below. For the sake of driving the point home, I will call these limitations "evil matches". I believe that these evil matches are planned from hell for the purpose of frustrating and aborting God's plans in peoples' lives. Many people take them as coincidence, but they are not. It is also hard to suspect that something wrong is happening in someone's life without spiritual insights. Before I share how to deal with evil matches, let me mention some of the evil matches or unusual scenarios that are common in peoples' lives.

## BLESSED BUT SORROWFUL

*The blessing of the Lord makes rich, and he adds no sorrow with it* (Proverbs 10:22, ESV).

Blessings and sorrow are not meant to go together. The blessings of God do not bring sorrow but peace and joy. If what you call blessing in your life is the source or the cause of your sorrows, then it is an evil match that needs correction. When God blesses a man, He blesses him to enjoy the blessing. God is a loving and a caring Father who wishes His children well. He wants them to be happy and to enjoy life in righteousness. Have you seen a person who has everything that people desire to have in life, but is ever sorrowful? From the outside he looks okay but in his closet, he wishes he were dead.

I talked to a young man who was brought up in a "good" family. He grew up lacking nothing. Since the father was a prominent man in the government, the children had a driver to take them to school and back. I admired him so much, especially when I thought of how my primary and secondary school years were.

I had to work in people's gardens to raise money for my uniform and upkeep. In the 10 years of my primary education, I never wore a pair of shoes to school, let alone being driven to school. And not withstanding my small body stature, I had to carry my school box back home from boarding school every closing day, and during half term, because the beddings I used in school were the same ones I used at home.

I was shocked when this young man I admired told me he wished the wasn't born in his family. While I wished I had been born there, he wished for the exact opposite. In tears, he narrated his story of how as children, they were helpless and could only watch as their mother was physically and emotionally abused, yet could do nothing about it because he was "connected". It was then that I realized that from the outside we saw what seemed like blessings, yet the young man was in chronic pain. Any time you find sorrow in your life that is almost continuous, it is an indicator of an evil match that needs to be corrected.

# RICH BUT LACKING AN HEIR

God blesses us with riches so that we can be generous to humanity in different ways. At the same time, one is not truly rich if whatever he has will die with him. The joy of every good father is to pass a legacy to his children. "A good person leaves an inheritance for their children's children" (Proverbs 10:32). It becomes an evil match when one is blessed with riches but he has no children to inherit his riches.

This situation does not just address those who have no biological children, but also those who have children but the enemy has stolen them. Many parents cry in pain when they see that they are rich but their children are lost in drugs and alcoholism, or have wasted their life in reckless living. The devil does this to kill a generation and to frustrate parents in order for them to drop the parental baton and in the process, lose the battle. No matter how hard the enemy has fought your generation, no matter how you feel about your heir, there is hope and an answer in Jesus.

Abraham was rich but didn't have an heir. He must have noted an evil match so he cried to God for help. "'Sovereign LORD, what good are all your blessings when I don't even have a son? Since you've given me no children, Eliezer of Damascus, a servant in my household, will inherit all my wealth. You have given me no descendants of my own, so one of my servants will be my heir.' Then the LORD said to him, 'No, your servant will not be your heir, for you will have a son of your own who will be your heir.'" (Genesis 15:2).

It is also equally painful when a man is blessed with an heir but has nothing to give as an inheritance, nothing to pass on to the next generation.

# MY PRAYER FOR YOU

*May God give you wealth and an heir to inherit your riches. May your wealth pass to the next generation and just like the scepter never left Judah, may your generation never lack an heir. May the Lord guard you and the generations after you.*

*Amen.*

## LACKING THE POWER TO ENJOY YOUR WEALTH

"There is an evil which I have seen under the sun and it is prevalent among men—a man to whom God has given riches and wealth and honor so that his soul lacks nothing of all that he desires; yet God has not empowered him to eat from them, for a foreigner enjoys them. This is vanity and a severe affliction" (Ecclesiastes 6:1-2, NASB).

It is an evil match for a man to be wealthy, yet he cannot enjoy his wealth. Consider a man who has enough money, even to buy a plane, but he cannot travel in it because he has a fear of heights. Or one who builds a lovely house but cannot sleep there because of insecurity. How about a person with a nice gigantic bed but cannot enjoy sleep because of the worries of this world? Even worse, you have money to buy any food you want, but the devil sends sickness into your body, with doctors advising you not to eat the very food you crave? These are evil matches that should be corrected.

# Having Wisdom but Remaining Poor

Wisdom that comes from God leads to wealth.

When Solomon asked God for wisdom, God told him that He would give him wealth also (1 Kings 3:13). Daniel was a wise man; he interpreted the dream of the king and received a promotion in addition to being clothed in purple and becoming wealthy (Daniel 2:48). Wisdom and poverty, I believe, is an evil match.

"There was once a small city with only a few people in it. And a powerful king came against it, surrounded it and built huge siege works against it. Now there lived in that city a man poor but wise, and he saved the city by his wisdom. But nobody remembered that poor man" (Ecclesiastes 9:14-15). Wisdom should match with riches and not poverty. Wisdom should make a person rich.

When Joseph interpreted Pharaoh's dream, he told him of the seven years of plenty and another seven of lack. Joseph then went ahead to recommend to Pharaoh to get a man of wisdom and put him in charge of the harvest with a charge: to save a fifth from all the proceeds of the land for use in the time of drought. This made Pharaoh so rich in the years of lack that he ended up buying back the whole land of Egypt (Genesis 41).

The wisdom of Joseph also got him to power, riches, and eventually saved his own family. Wisdom is God-given and so are riches. This particular evil match works to deny people the pay for their labor. It also attracts injustices. The poor man who saved the king in Ecclesiastes 9:14-15 should have been rewarded for the good job, but see how poverty denied him the honor that was his.

There are so many people who are suffering in hospitals, prisons, etc., because they are poor. Some have gone through life's injustices because of poverty. No matter how righteous or wise you are, if you are poor, some injustice will be meted against you.

In July 2016 I was preaching in Church Eleven32 in Texas about dealing with evil matches; I asked the congregation whether my preaching blessed them, and they said yes. I asked them to raise their hands if they believed I am saved and cannot steal. Many hands went up. I then posed a question to them: "If, say, Bill Gates and I visited your house: Gates as a wealthy businessman and myself as a man of God. Then in excitement, you step out of your house to buy some milk, and when you come back, find we have left, and your television is missing. Who would be your first suspect?"

I was not surprised at how unanimously I became the suspect. The anointing I had demonstrated as I preached and prayed for the needs of people could not save me. Bill Gates might not have been as holy or anointed as I was, but he was wealthy.

My anointing was challenged just as the wisdom of the poor man was despised and forgotten because of poverty.

## How to Deal With Evil Matches

To know whether or not evil matches are manifest in your life, it is important to do personal introspection and research. A simple survey can reveal many things. Some things may appear ordinary, yet can be very spiritual. For example, family history should not be ignored.

When an expectant mother goes for her prenatal clinic, the doctor usually asks questions (do you have a history of high blood pressure in your family? Do you know of any twin births in your family?)

to form a medical opinion. The answers help to determine if there might be a pattern the doctor needs to note, and perhaps prevent or arrest. Some evil matches can be generational and easily hang on the ignorance of believers.

Jabez must have done some research to know what happened during his birth. Perhaps he talked to a midwife or a woman of his mother's age who told him the story. A keen observation in one's life can reveal some contradicting patterns or occurrences, as I shared earlier, that can be seen as a potential evil match.

You do not carry out research for the sake of knowledge only, but to deal with the results. Once an evil match is identified, the first thing one must do is pray; not just any other prayer, but prayer that is on target. The prayer of Jabez is a model prayer for dealing with evil matches.

We have seen that one way of dealing with evil matches is through prayer. The second way is by believing in the word of the servants of God. One thing that the devil has tried to do, and has been gaining ground on, is to make people lose their faith in their spiritual leaders. God has always used his servants to lead and direct his people. The Bible tells us to have faith in God and His prophets. "Believe firmly in God, your God, and your lives will be firm! Believe in your prophets and you'll come out on top" (2 Chronicles 20:20, MSG).

At one church, after talking about people believing in their prophets, a congregant followed me after the service and said that what I had talked about was Old Testament theology, which has no place in the New Testament. He derived his argument from Matthew 27:51, when the curtain of the temple was torn from top to bottom. His argument was Jesus Christ replaced the priesthood of human beings, thus, there was no more need for priests or prophets. Many people hold that view and thus despise their spiritual authority.

Look at this New Testament verse, "He…filled earth with his gifts. He handed out gifts of apostle, prophet, evangelist, and pastor-teacher" (Ephesians 4:11, MSG). This tells us that God has given his prophets power to prosper his people and to speak against evil matches as God directs them.

When Elisha sent word to Naaman that he should go and wash in the River Jordan seven times, he was not happy. He thought the prophet, at the very least, would wave his hands over his body (2 Kings 5:11). Later, when he obeyed the divine instructions he was healed. For one to obey the word of a servant of God, he must believe in him first.

A case of an evil match was brought to Prophet Elisha. The people of the city said to Elisha, "Look, our Lord, this town is well situated… but the water is bad and the land is unproductive" (2 Kings 2:19). Those people came to Elisha because they believed in him.

"Then he went out to the source of the water, and cast in the salt there, and said, "Thus says the Lord: 'I have healed this water; from it there shall be no more death or barrenness.' So the water remains healed to this day, according to the word of Elisha which he spoke" (2 Kings 2:21-22, NKJV).

The work of a servant of God is to make decrees. For those decrees to work for the people, they must have faith in their prophets and in the declarations made. The water remains healed to this day as per the word of Elisha, not God. This tells me that God allowed Elisha to represent Him.

# PRAYER

*Heavenly Father in the name of Jesus, I pray against any evil match that may have controlled me. May I align my life to your plan and will. Give me the strength to enjoy every blessing you give to me. I will not be identified with pain or lack. May my relationship with you keep growing stronger and stronger with each passing day.*

*Amen.*

# CHAPTER TEN

# The Wisdom of Saving & Investing

The *Canadian Students' Dictionary* defines investment as, committing (money or capital) in order to gain profit or interest, as by purchasing property or securities; or utilizing money for future advantage or benefit.

A savings plan should always have a good investment plan otherwise it is merely postponed expenditure.

An old man once told me that saving starts when one's stomach is full. This is the way many people think. They believe that they have nothing to save. Saving is a discipline; if one waits to have extra money or a certain time in the future to begin to save, that money and time will never come.

In martial arts, they say you have not graduated if you have not developed a third eye. The third eye enables you to see without turning towards the enemy who approaches from the back. In the same way, unless you develop the discipline to save from whatever amount you receive, whether large or small, you will never grow your financial muscle income, whether small or big, there is a savings; it is not possible to save. We should always have a plan about what to do with the money that remains after giving our tithes and offerings to God.

There is no magic behind giving 10% and prospering. I believe in tithing, but I also know that what you do with the 90% that remains in your hands is equally important in the process of dealing with financial strongholds. God says, "*…and when they drink deadly poison, it will not hurt them at all*" (Mark 16:18). Does this mean that we ought to look for poison and drink? Of course, not. In the same way, the Bible does not mean that when we give our tithes, we ought to eat our 90% and sleep as God releases wealth and riches to us. God expects us to save and invest what remains after giving our tithes and offerings.

## THE JOSEPH PRINCIPLE

The savings and investment plan I will share with you is what I call the Joseph Principle. Joseph interpreted Pharaoh's dream then went ahead to share the wisdom of saving with him.

> *Let Pharaoh appoint commissioners over the land to take a fifth of the harvest of Egypt during the seven years of abundance. They should collect all the food of these good years that are coming and store up the grain under the authority of Pharaoh, to be kept in the cities for food. This food should be held in reserve for the country, to be used during the seven years of famine that will come upon Egypt, so that the country may not be ruined by the famine* (Genesis 41:34-36).

In the Joseph Principle, one saves 20% of all their income. I know that 20% may seem too little or too much depending on individual circumstances, but it can achieve a lot. The Bible records that when famine came, people from far nations came to buy food in Egypt. Egypt was a monopoly as far as food was concerned. Joseph made a lot of money for the king and the kingdom. The little 20% saved many lives from death, and made Pharaoh very rich.

The second thing that happened was that Joseph used the 20% he had saved to buy all the land of Egypt back for Pharaoh. When the people had spent their money and livestock, the only thing they could call theirs was land. So they came and sold it for food to Joseph. They said:

> *"Why should we perish before your eyes—we and our land as well? Buy us and our land in exchange for food, and we with our land will be in bondage to Pharaoh. Give us seed so that we may live and not die"…So Joseph bought all the land in Egypt for Pharaoh. The Egyptians, one and all, sold their fields, because the famine was too severe for them. The land became Pharaoh's, and Joseph reduced the people to servitude, from one end of Egypt to the other* (Genesis 47:20-21).

## APPLYING THE JOSEPH PRINCIPLE

### FIRST, DON'T WAIT TO HAVE ENOUGH TO SAVE

I mentioned earlier that many of us, especially in our African context, were taught to spend and not to save because savings are supposed to be from leftovers. Purpose to save as soon as you receive your income, whether it is little or much, whether you have needs or not. It is doable. It worked for Joseph and it can work for you too.

## SECOND, SAVE IN AN OPAQUE BAG

One of the reasons farmers put pesticide on maize or other seeds is to make sure they are not tempted to eat the seed put aside for the next planting season. If you save your money where it is easily accessible, you can be sure you will keep spending it. The solution is to keep your money in an "opaque bag" where you can't get it with ease. Put your money in an account that has some limitations or some penalties for withdrawal. You can also invest your 20% as it comes in short-term investment avenues that you access for better investment ideas.

## INVEST IN ASSETS THAT APPRECIATE IN VALUE

Such assets include land or commercial buildings. The risk in land or building is not as high as in livestock or even some stocks. It doesn't matter where that land is; land is land. Of course you must do due diligence when you are purchasing the land, so you are not conned out of your hard-earned savings.

When I first tried the Joseph Principle, it was really difficult. I would start, but after a few months I could not keep the discipline. Later, I promised myself that I would do it. I am happy to say I have been able to make some good progress and the results are amazing.

If you are accountable to yourself and to God, and practice these principles, you will marvel at what you can achieve with what you have. Financial breakthrough means being able to manage whatever God has put in your hands.

# MY PRAYER FOR YOU

*May the Lord give you the courage to save and the wisdom to invest in the right place. Like Isaac, may your investment give you a hundredfold return because the Lord blesses you (Genesis 26:12).*

*Amen.*

# CHAPTER ELEVEN

# SERVE GOD WITH MONEY

*You can't serve God and money, but you can serve God*
*with money.*
Selwyn Hughes

## START WITH THE BREAK-EVEN POINT (BEP)

I describe BEP as that point where costs of a commodity are met, and beyond it, profits are realized. It is hard to arrive at a BEP in the matters of God. It is not easy to locate the point where one feels they can tell how much tithe they have spent in the kingdom of God and can now begin to enjoy profit or "recover" their money.

Before giving or investing in God, one must start with the BEP. To start with the BEP means to have it clear in one's mind that they have no money of their own and so what they spend for the kingdom already belongs to God. I share this because I know there are many people are God's creditors. They have "loaned" God so much money and feel He has not settled their debt yet. When this mentality controls someone, it becomes very hard to break financial strongholds. It is important to understand that before we get any wealth, we belong to God and when we have it, both we, and the wealth we possess, belong to Him.

In our path to breaking financial strongholds, God gives talents or assignments or responsibilities to us, for which we shall give an account.

When God called me into full-time ministry, I had almost nothing in terms of financial resources. In fact, I would say I had more faith than money. I took over leadership of a church that was in debt, with a membership of less than a hundred people who took too long to adjust and adapt to the transition. The church was also involved in a land ownership court battle, which we had to service for a long time. The land rates had not been paid for more than 10 years and I had to clear the outstanding amount. It was a hard season, especially as a new leader.

Though I had no money to handle all these matters, God was on my side, and today I look back and thank Him. I went without a salary for a long duration. There were bills to pay and people who needed and expected financial support from me, but which was not available. I also had people who never believed in me. When I look at what I have achieved, I remind myself I had nothing of my own except that God was on my side. There is nothing to tell of our break-even point. All I used then belonged to God, and all I use now still belongs to God.

When a person has spent on a cause and he awaits to receive a re-ward, that is his or her BEP. Depending on the area of interest, the break-even point will vary. In a pure business set-up, this point is a lot clearer than in a church. You can keep a record of your expen-diture and match against your turnover, and you can tell when the profit starts coming in. In a church set-up, the story is different.

I have sympathized with pastors especially the pioneers of a ministry, when they are accused of lacking financial integrity. When one is starting a church, he or she invests all they have in the ministry. Many times there is no difference between personal money and church money. Many pastors have given what their children and spouse would have used, for the benefit of the church. The reality has been that at the initial stages, many pastors begin with no money and sometimes no members. As the church starts to grow, members and money start coming in. In a short while, as members begin to own the church, they demand more accountability. At this time, if the leader is not well prepared, he or she ends up fighting the people and sometimes demolishing whatever they have built over a long period of time.

It is at this stage, if the church is not careful, it can lose both money and the pastor. This is when people start talking about "our money" and the pastor can end up feeling hurt. This is also the time when the pastor probably feels that the return for his or her labor has finally come. In fact they quote the Bible saying, "The elders who perform their leadership duties well are to be considered worthy of double honor (financial support), especially those who work hard at preaching and teaching [the word of God concerning eternal salvation through Christ]" (1 Timothy 5:17, AMP); but on the contrast, the members feel it is time to protect their giving.

Of course, both the pastor and the members are right. Indeed it is true that the pastor needs to be appreciated for the effort and sacrifice he or she put in the church or ministry. He is deserving of a reward. Members too have a right to ask for accountability of the money they give.

It is at this stage when you may hear statements from a pastor such as:

- I invested all my life in this church; nobody has the right to question me.

- Where were you when I was suffering alone?

- What is wrong even if I take all the money? After all, I have suffered enough in the ministry.

- If God has entrusted your hearts to me, why can't you trust me with your pockets?

To be honest, I feel for these pastors and I can tell you that indeed church planting can be a draining process. However, they need to get to a place of breaking even. A BEP in church terms is not a place where expenses meet other costs, but a place where one accepts that you gave your all because God gave it to you. You started that work because God called you to do it. This is the point to acknowledge the achievements made are all by the grace of God. Until one gets to this place in life, it will be impossible to talk of financial breakthrough especially in ministry.

If you have ever started a business or any other venture, you know making sacrifices is a requisite. You should not look back and begin to regret the lost or missed opportunities as you worked to establish your venture. Let me add here that any labor in the Lord does not go unnoticed by Him. That said, there are three powerful things we should never forget as we serve God with our money:

**THE GOD OF THE VISION IS THE GOD OF PROVISION**

There is no man who can receive a vision from God and provide for it. God's projects are huge and require a lot of resources. No single person can provide for them. If a man or woman purports to have a vision from God that he or she single-handedly provides for, he or she is a liar. One can have money but cannot supply the grace needed. A person can have money, but money is not the only resource needed to achieve a God-given vision.

God provides whatever we give in the ministry, for it is His work. This means we have nothing to give to God if He does not give to us first. Instead of focusing on the money we have invested, we should view ourselves as stewards who are doing what the Lord commands. I have nothing of my own. I am a steward of God's property. This attitude has helped me give without counting. "…When you have done everything you were told to do, you should say, "We are unworthy servants; we have only done our duty" (Luke 17:10).

## GOD REWARDS

In my book, *Called to Serve,* I have talked about the vertical blessings of a servant. Giving is a bless- ing when the giver has the attitude that whatever leaves his hands is received by God. This means that anything I give to people or to the church, God will reward me. Without this attitude, it is easy to carry a "record" of your giving and the debts that God "owes" you. No wonder, then, when you don't receive in the same measure you are giving you get disappointed or annoyed. This is because you never got to a place of realizing that if you gave to God, you can rest assured that you have His sure reward. This calls for spiritual sensitivity to enable us hear God's voice and discern His will, on what to receive and what not to receive from people.

I once prayed for a woman who had been in a coma for more than four years. As we stepped out of the house with my friend Bobby, the husband of the lady we had prayed for followed us. He reached into his pocket to give me some money which he insisted I should take. I sensed in my heart God did not want me to take the money. So, I thanked him and told him not to worry about the money because I had come to bless him. Later, Bobby asked me why I did not take the money and I told him that if I had taken the money, I would have received my pay from man, but by refusing the money, I was giving God a chance to reward me.

The very next day, a gentleman I had met a while back, and who had heard I was in the area, said to me, "I am sorry I have not been able to attend your meeting; tell me, what would you like me to do for you?" I quickly gave him my immediate wish list and to my surprise, he brought to my hotel room two items, both worth over $5,000, which was more than what the husband of the lady we prayed for would have removed from his wallet. God indeed rewards us, let us give Him a chance.

## THE RIGHT ATTITUDE TOWARDS WEALTH

For one to break their financial limitation, they must have the right attitude towards wealth, money, and riches. Some people are poor because of their wrong attitude towards riches. One cannot receive what they criticize. The ministry in which I serve is located within a relatively poor neighborhood. One thing I have noted over the years is that the poor are more comfortable with the poor. Poverty can unite people like the ten lepers who were united by their condition (Luke 17:11-19).

In the book, *A Time to Prosper*, Chuck Pierce and Robert Heidler say, "Christians should view wealth as a resource intended for the advancement of God's kingdom… We must not fear what God has given us to harvest. We must not fear increase, for money in itself is not bad."

We don't serve God for money but we need money to serve God. This should be our attitude. Those who fight others for teaching or preaching about prosperity or money end up in poverty. The truth is, anything we oppose, criticize or have a wrong attitude towards will repel us, and so if we oppose wealth or riches or money, it will repel us.

# CHAPTER TWELVE

# TRUTHS AND HALF-TRUTHS ABOUT MONEY

As we work at having the right attitude and seek to break financial strongholds, it is important to correct the following half-truths and truths about money.

## MONEY IS EVIL

Many people have picked this statement and have argued that it is scriptural. The Bible has no verse that says money is evil. 2 Timothy 6:10 says, *For the love of money is a root of all kinds of evil* (NASB).

Two things stand out for me from this verse. First, "the love of money"; money is not evil but the love of it may attract evil. This does not in any way say one should keep off money. The Bible says keep off the love of it. If the desire to have money overtakes someone, evil comes in. Because of the love of money, people have stolen or even killed.

Second, the article "a" before "root of all kinds of evil" means the love of money is one of the roots of evil and not the only one. There are many other roots of evil and just as we must be careful not to sin against God by loving money, we must also work not to sin against Him by doing other things that are evil in His sight. In other words, we must not think that love of money is "the" but "a" root of all kinds of evil.

Those who think money is evil will find it hard to serve God or achieve much for Him. You need money to serve God.

## THE RICH ARE DEVIL WORSHIPPERS

This may sound funny but it is truly the belief of some. Many people have a problem with money and riches because of the picture that is painted through the preaching of the wrong doctrine, that money belongs to the devil.

Some people associate riches with devil worship and poverty with holiness. They believe that the poorer a person is, the closer they are to God. This, I would say, is one of the many errors that King Solomon saw under the sun. People have been made to believe that money belongs to the devil. People have no problem seeing a bar or brothel packed with people who are driving nice vehicles, yet they have a problem when they see a church and its ministers prospering.

For one to deal with this attitude, it is important to understand what God says about his children. The word of God is our canon and so it should be given a chance to inform us. In the wake of what is branded as the "prosperity gospel", a lot has been said and done. There are those who believe in the prosperity gospel and those who don't.

A university student writing a paper on the balanced gospel, citing the rising of the prosperity gospel and preachers of the same, once interviewed me. I could tell that the student was not for the prosperity gospel or its preachers. After talking with him for some time,

I realized he needed my support in criticizing what he saw as a vice, rather than my objective contribution to his scholarly paper. I told him that I believe in the wholistic teachings found in the Bible and as long as the Bible talks about the prosperity of the children of God, then I would have no problem with that teaching.

The Bible tells me that silver and gold is the Lord's (Haggai 2:8). The earth and its possession is God's, cattle on a thousand hills are His (Psalm 50:10). The God we serve is rich. Since like begets like, then it is impossible for a child of God to be poor. Poverty is of the devil but riches and wealth are of our God. It is important for a Christian to know that Christ became poor so that we can be rich.

Paul prayed that the Philippians would be blessed according to the riches of his glory in Christ Jesus (Philippians 4:19). These Scriptures confirm to me that my Father is a rich Father and that He is happy when we prosper, as His children.

## RICHES OR MONEY WILL TAKE YOU AWAY FROM THE WILL OF GOD

Many people have the wrong perception about God and money. There are those who believe that being poor means that you are closer to God. Job's story is different, he was wealthy and great, yet blameless and upright, a man who feared God and shunned *evil* (Job 1:1-3). Others feel that the more money you have, the closer your relationship with God is because you are blessed. I am of the opinion that it is more honorable to represent God in riches than in poverty.

## MONEY TRUTHS

Here are two fundamental truths I have discovered about money:

## MONEY FOLLOWS PROJECTS

There is enough money on earth to do everything that needs doing on earth. There is a pastor I admire and respect. He is zealous for the Lord and at peace serving Him. One day he invited me to his house for lunch. When I visited, I got to know he not only owned the property but was also a landlord.

At the time, I was heavily in debt, and my ministry did not seem like it would ever grow. I decided to ask him to help me get rich. This is what he said, "Have a daily project, a weekly project, a monthly project, and a yearly project for both your family and church." He concluded his advice like this, "Money follows a project. Money not attached to a project is money on transit, and it will go where there are projects."

Since I received this advice, I have never stayed without a project. I have learned that ten dollars in the hands of a person with no project is a plate of food, but the same in the hands of one with a project is a bag of cement.

I challenge you to have projects or goals you are working towards, and you are on your way to financial freedom and wealth. Praying for money when you have no goal is like praying for the rain, yet you have nowhere to plant.

## MONEY FOLLOWS RISK-TAKERS

If you fear losing you will not be rich. Many rich people were called failures at some point, but they never gave up. Risk-takers are not afraid of failure. Many Christians want to invest when God has given them the clear sign and confirmation that they will get profit. But whoever watches the wind will not plant; whoever looks at the clouds will not reap (Ecclesiastes 11:4). We must overcome the fear of failure and take calculated risks, if we will make it.

## MONEY FOLLOWS CREATIVITY AND IMAGINATION

Money does not necessarily follow education but creativity and imagination. You do not have to be corrupt or crafty to be rich—you only need to exercise creativity. Don't just pray, sit and think creatively about a problem you would like to solve, and you will be on your way to financial freedom.

## MONEY IS LIKE LIQUID

Money takes the shape of the container it is put in. In other words, money is a humble and obedient servant. Money does not give a person value; it is the understanding of its owner that gives it value. A child given a hundred dollar note will not treat the money in the same way a grown-up would. It is the same with two adults would. Therefore, master your money and it will work for you to help you achieve your goals.

## MY PRAYER FOR YOU

*May you never miss your blessing of wealth and riches because of wrong beliefs. May you remain committed to God even as you become rich and wealthy. Like Job, may you be called blameless and upright, fearing the God, and shunning evil.*

*Amen.*

# CONCLUSION

Nobody has a monopoly of knowledge, and that is why no single book or person can handle the issues of money single-handedly. As the Bible says, we prophesy in part (1 Corinthians 13:9); I have just shared my part of the knowledge, experience, and revelation from God on how to deal with finances. I have tried to put it down in the simplest way possible, so that whatever your financial status and background, you may understand the principles and spiritual insights on how to break financial strongholds or limitations.

As you have read through the pages of this book, I pray you have been inspired to change your attitude and practice towards money. Any journey, even a financial one, begins with a single step. Don't be afraid to take it, as you commit yourself to God who is your helper. I know there are people who are agents of the devil, whose mandate is to hold the wealth of the believers in every spiritual way possible. May God force them to release your wealth in Jesus name. *He will spit out the riches he swallowed; God will make his stomach vomit them* (Job 20:15).

*For you know the grace of our Lord Jesus Christ, that though he was rich, yet for your sake he be- came poor, so that you through his poverty might become rich (2 Corinthians 8:9).*

*I declare in the name of Jesus that I am in the new covenant of the blood of Jesus, which is a covenant of riches and not poverty. You took away my poverty and gave me riches. Any voice that speaks poverty I silence it in the name of Jesus Christ.*

*Amen.*

## PRAYER

**Father in the name of Jesus Christ, You created me to prosper and allocated my share of wealth for me to enjoy while I live on earth. I now take charge over my finances, my wealth, and my treasures. Anybody who is holding them now, I command in the name of Jesus to release them. Those who have swallowed my resources and wealth, according to your word, let them vomit it in Jesus' name.**

**Amen.**

# NOTES

"92 Quotes About Debt that'll Make You think, Laugh, & Tweet!".
*Manvsdebt.com.* 2017.

Greene, Robert. *The 48 Laws of Power.* New York: Penguin Books, 2000.

Herring, Harold. 2017. "7 Keys to Your Financial Breakthrough". *Haroldherring.Com.* https://haroldherring.com/ blogs/harolds-blogs/life-strategies/1215-7-keys-to-you r-financial- breakthrough.

Kiyosaki, Robert T. and Sharon L. Lechter. *Rich Dad's Cashflow Quadrant.* New York: Warner Books, 2003.

Oyedepo, David O. *Success Strategies: Putting In Your Hand The Scriptural Password To Unending Success.* Okeja, Lagos, Nigeria: Dominion Publishing House, 2003.

Oyedepo, David O. *Understanding Financial Prosperity.* Okeja, Lagos, Nigeria: Dominion Publishing House, 1997.

Pierce, Chuck D. and Robert Heidler. *A Time To Prosper.* United States: Chosen Books, 2013.

Pringle, Phil. *Keys To Financial Excellence*. New Kensington: Whitaker House, 2008.

Robbins, Dale. 2017. "Breaking Spiritual Strongholds". *Dale A Robbins*. http://victorious.org/pub/breaking-strongholds-141.

Rush, Myron. *God's Business*. Colorado Springs: Victor, 2002.

Strand, Robert J. *Before The Offering Is Received*. Mobile: Evergreen Press, 2016.

Tongoi, Dennis O. *Mixing God With Money*. Nairobi, Kenya: Bezalel Investments Ltd., 2002.

Ziglar, Zig. *Zig Ziglar's Life Lifters*. Nashville, Tennessee: Broadman & Holman, 2003.

Apostle Patrick Murithii Nyaga is the lead minister of the Gospel Celebration Church, Nairobi. He trained and worked as an accountant before joining full-time ministry. Patrick holds a Bachelor of Arts in Bible and Theology degree from Pan Africa Christian University. In addition to his role as a lead minister, he is also a global conference speaker and regularly contributes articles in the Leadership Journal and Leadership Today Africa. He also has a television program, "Called to Serve" on Kingdom Television, in Kenya. Patrick is married to Grace, and they are blessed with three children, Jewel, Moses, and Collins.

*Leadership Pitfalls: Mistakes Every Leader Must Avoid*

*Called To Serve: A Biblical Invitation to Serve Sacrificialluy*

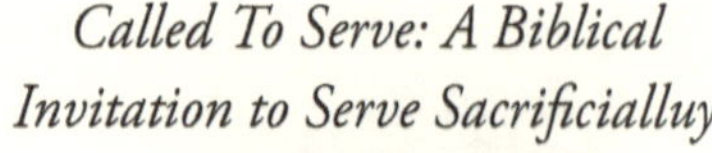

*Leadership Pitfalls: Mistakes Every Leader Must Avoid (Amharic Translation)*

*Every Leader's Battle: Experiences, Encouragement & Lessons from 10 Leaders*

*CALLED TO SERVE (Amharic Translation)*